Handbook
for Light Ambassadors

by

Peter Schmuck
and
Richard Grawath

We dedicate this book to our ancestors
Anna Schmuck, her husband
and their 12 children.

Contents

Why This Book?

Many people feel that today's patterns of life in the industrialised countries cannot continue for much longer. We depend on raw materials that are running out. We do not share the fruits of our labour fairly. In many places, wars and disputes flare up again and again, mostly over the limited resources that are still available - over water, over natural gas or oil, over fertile soil.

Will these disputes continue or perhaps even intensify because raw materials are becoming scarcer? Or will the current century bring about a turning point for us humans? Will we invent and try out new ways of living that are based on the fruits of our earth, which grow back year after year and use sunlight and wind so that energy flows are used that nature makes available to us? Will we learn to distribute these fruits and energies more fairly than is customary today? Will we learn to live in respect and compassion with all beings on planet Earth?

This handbook is written for people who have asked themselves these questions but do not yet have satisfactory answers. We intend to guide you through a process of self-discovery in a world of great change. The old world has been deliberately crashed by a small group of super rich people who want to increase the concentration of power and assets in their control.

As a result, more and more people realise that a reversal will come from the bottom and middle sections of society.

This handbook provides assistance in identifying opportunities and roles for individuals in a process of change which will lead to a fairer and more humane future. In addition, it is intended to support discussions in groups which want to do grass-roots projects.

We largely avoid the terminology of the dying society because it is used in a manipulative manner in order to convert weaknesses into alleged strengths. The Human Development Index (HDI) and Gross Domestic Product (GDP) are two examples of misleading key indicators for "development".

Instead we do our best, relying on simple and precise language, to give a concise overview regarding three topics: (1) Diagnosis of the status quo: Why is the old structure of society obsolete and what is the breeding ground for the emerging society? (2) Options: Where are the points of origin for the world we want? Which human potentials are needed in the emerging society? (3) My next steps: How can I find the right people and my place in the emerging society, regarding spiritual and material aspects?

We invite you, by reading this book, to go through a process of discovery as we reflect, detect and develop our human potential for creating and supporting a happy, fair and clean world. The emerging society will replace the dark powers of the old world which contaminated our air, sky, soil, water and minds. Becoming a Light Ambassador - is that not a great goal?

First Step: Diagnosis

We invite you to start with a short diagnosis of the dying society and the potentials of the emerging one. Doing such a diagnosis is not trivial because the crash of the old system is not presented by the established mass media which present only a small part of the actual economic and political issues in our world from a perspective favourable to the small ruling group of people in charge.

At first glance media companies, large corporations and NGOs often appear to be separate entities but in reality they are a tightly knit network of a few individuals. Alternative sources for information are therefore required for an appropriate diagnosis. Examples of alternative sources of information will be provided later in this handbook.

Through these sources we get an overview of the old world's leaders' goals and formulate the emerging world's guidelines. We finish the diagnosis chapter with a look at human, psychological and spiritual potentials which enable the unfolding of the emerging society.

The Dying and the Emerging Society

In nature there is a wonderful analogy for societal change during which a dying society is replaced by an emerging society.

Do you know how butterflies come to be? It is widely known that butterflies emerge from caterpillars. Do you know the fascinating details of this process?

The caterpillar stage comes to an end when the caterpillar pupates. The first cells of the developing butterfly, the so-called imago cells, appear in the pupa. The caterpillar's immune system repels these imago cells because its immune system tries to defend the current stage of development. For a while the caterpillar's body can successfully destroy the imago cells. The situation changes when clusters of the imago cells form within the dying body of the caterpillar. These clusters gather together through fine threads until the caterpillar's defence system collapses.

The fascinating development continues as the pupa forms a rigid, solid shell from which the mature butterfly emerges through a process which demands much energy. If one tries to skip this process by opening the pupa from the outside, the hatched butterfly will not be able to fly. You can read more about the details of these events in the work of Norie Huddle (1990).

In terms of societal change, could it be that a dying structure is simply unable to anticipate or even welcome a new society? Their representatives repeat like a mantra, "There is no alternative." Could they be fighting the new structures? Might it be that the dying dark forces finally clear the way as soon as enough Light Ambassadors or imago cells have come together?

Let us try to find out why the old society is dying. In the future this may help us avoid mistakes which led to the downfall of political structures which were initially democratic and legal.

Among the human attempts to achieve paradise on our planet there are three major visions which have had an impact on our life patterns in several countries over decades and even centuries.

(1) The Christian religion has exerted great influence in many countries for two millennia. (2) Marxism developed a vision of communism, firstly

formulated in 1848, which in the 20th century became the state doctrine of some countries in Eastern Europe, Asia, Africa, Central and South America. (3) Sustainability was first formulated in 1713 by the German forest scientist Hans Carl von Carlowitz* as a forestry principle according to which no more trees should be felled than can grow back. This vision culminated in 1992 in a global declaration of intent by almost all leading politicians in the world: Agenda 21*. This was a blueprint for building a new societal structure.

All three visions failed. Do you agree? But did we learn enough from these experiences to restart our awakening to paradise today? We are convinced that the time has now come for a big new adventure for humanity. We invite you to look back to the lessons learned from our past. These are the basis of our optimism for the actual transformation of humanity.

What are the common themes of the above-mentioned visions? Despite different terminology, we find the desire, the goal, the vision to be that we should treat each other fairly, that we should share equitably and that we should not harm other people.

In the modern variant of the sustainability vision, this fairness and respect are extended to living beings in general, i.e. also to non-human life such as animals and plants.

We know today that all three visions could not deliver what their inventors, disciples and followers aimed for. Let us reflect upon the reasons for the failure of these past great ideas.

(1) The vision with the longest history, the Christian religion, has morally discredited itself, even in the opinion of many "former" Christians. Crusades, crimes and wars exterminating whole peoples were carried out in the name of or with the toleration of the leadership of the Christian church. The Spanish inquisition is one such well known example.

(2) The vision of Marxism may be regarded as historically outdated. One of the authors lived for 33 years under a communist regime, experiencing personally the hypocrisy and mendacity of the communist leaders in East Germany. Consequently, almost all state structures with a corresponding ideological doctrine have collapsed and the original basic ideas are no longer pursued in the few that still

do exist. Kolakowski, a Polish scientist analysed the reasons for that decay (1981).

(3) The vision of sustainability, intended to give a political orientation function in our world in 1992 as Agenda 21*, has actually been reduced to absurdity. Even in countries such as Germany where a sustainability council advises the government, more land today is covered in concrete than in 1992 and concrete covered areas are increasing further. Soil fertility and biodiversity continue to decrease, differences in income continue to increase, and opencast mines continue to victimise entire villages. Globally, too, it can be stated that more people today are starving and malnourished than in 1992 and that the forest area is decreasing.

The reasons for the failure of this vision are, again, hypocrisy and mendacity. The old system's leaders proposed creating a fair and balanced world order, but instead they implemented measures which serve their own interests.

Let us look at two examples. Gross Domestic Product (GDP) is a figure which supposedly indicates a positive development when the figure increases. This can be criticised on the grounds that certain forms of private and governmental spending may be bad for whole populations. If a government spends huge amounts of money for weapons then this has devastating consequences for humans, animals and plants in times of war; however, the higher GDP indicates economic growth.

The Human Development Index (HDI) supposedly measures human development. The HDI is part of the United Nations Development Programme (UNDP). It is a composite index which contains various other measurements such as the GDP, the mean time of schooling and education programmes in a particular country. Most school systems around the globe, however, are based on the Prussian school system which was designed to produce obedient civil servants and soldiers. Are these guidelines appropriate for our new world? What do you think?

As a further example, Carlowitz's originally simple and productive idea of sustainability has been completely perverted by using this expression within actual programme papers of the World Economic Forum. Under the umbrella of sustainability, the authors of these papers associate genetic manipulation, steady economic growth, transhumanism and total digital surveillance, all of which are ethically contrary to the original idea of sustainability.

Can one conclude from these "accidents" in the history of our species that we humans are an incorrectly programmed being of evolution, an "evolutionary stray", as Arthur Köstler wrote back in 1978? Can one conclude that anyone who today still has visions should go to a psychiatrist, as a former German chancellor maintained?

At least two arguments make this conclusion appear premature and questionable. Our historical knowledge based on old written texts suggests that the period of unjust social conditions lasted for a few thousand years. This is only the lifetime of a few dozen generations.

For most of the history of our evolution as a species, spanning hundreds of thousands of years and thus many thousands of generations, during which our hereditary factors have been formed, we have had to rely on conjecture in assessing the lives of these ancestors.

There are many arguments to suggest that

humans could only survive in groups and are therefore essentially social beings. Probably many people of all generations lived in respect for and reference to their ambient world. We assume this from, amongst other things, the remains of shamanistically orientated cultures.

How was it possible that the former balance between justice amongst humans and respect for creation was upset during the last few millennia? Why have the great visions not yet led to success? Might it be that our ancestors followed misleading basic assumptions regarding the distribution of power in their societies? We will take a closer look at that idea later.

The other argument that offers us grounds for hope derives from misconceptions about long periods of time. Ten thousand years ago the agricultural revolution brought about the first global changes caused by humans. The above-mentioned problem-solving theories span a period of about 2,000 years. Such short periods are modest compared to the time taken for the development of our species, which took hundreds of thousands of years.

Is it not reasonable if we allow ourselves a few new attempts instead of giving up and burying the "best" and last of all societies with the current one?

According to the authors, the dying society is based upon misleading assumptions about our own psychological nature, about the design of our economic system and about patterns of distribution and consumption. These misleading assumptions or thinking traps, working as self-fulfilling prophecies, have given rise to the pathological patterns of life that prevail today.

1. The ego trap: "*We humans are above all ego-oriented and competition-driven beings.*"

2. The anthropocentrism trap: "*We humans are the most highly developed beings in evolution and have more rights than other living beings.*"

3. The consumption/happiness trap: "*Consumption makes people happy; a lot of money enables a lot of consumption and therefore this makes people particularly happy.*"

4. The interest trap: "*A monetary system with interest is necessary for an economy.*"

5. The growth trap: "*Continuous economic growth is*

necessary."

6. The resource trap: "*The resources available to us are in principle endless.*"

7. The centralisation trap: "C*entralised production is always better than distributed production.*"

8. The private property trap: "*Private ownership of public things serves to preserve them.*"

9. The opinion-forming trap: "*It is easy to form one's own accurate and purposeful opinion.*"

10. The meaning trap: "*It is trivial or not necessary to try to find the meaning of one's life.*"

A detailed description of the thinking traps and alternative solutions can be found in Schmuck (2015).

To give you an idea of the current economic situation, according to Advratings* the total value of assets under management (AUM) of the two largest fund management companies BlackRock and Vanguard in 2021 amounted to:

BlackRock:	USD	9, 500, 000, 000, 000
Vanguard:	USD	<u>8, 400, 000, 000, 000</u>
TOTAL:	**USD**	**17, 900, 000, 000, 000**

Yes, this is $17.9 trillion, a number that is hard for

us to fully comprehend. This amount for merely two firms is larger than the economic output (GDP) of every country on the planet other than the US (Statisticstimes*). In other words, the total value of all goods produced and services provided by every country except the US was smaller than the combined AUM of just the 2 top asset management firms (Statisticstimes*).

Furthermore, BlackRock and Vanguard hold shares in each other's companies. This indicates that coordinated actions (collusion) between these two as well as between other fund management firms are based upon shared interests. It is also likely if not highly probable that there is collusion by firms managing funds from the same industries or even from the same companies. The enormous amount of AUM suggests that the large asset management firms can easily move markets (influence prices) and moreover that these companies have the means to influence, pressure and/or even blackmail politicians and governments.

Where does this money come from? It includes the assets from small investors, their savings as well as their pension funds and life assurance policies.

Therefore if the majority of small investors were to pull their assets out of the large asset management companies as well as from the large banks and corporations then the ruling class would lose power, thereby making it easier to create a new, fair society.

Major macroeconomic changes took place after World War II. Corporate mergers and acquisitions led to a concentration of money and power in the hands of a few. The FIRE sector (Finance, Insurance and Real Estate) has come to dominate the scene.

In the wake of the Global Financial Crisis of 2008, governments transferred large amounts of money to the financial sector in the form of bail-outs to banks after those banks had speculated with the money of others and produced phenomenally large losses.

Germany is the economic power-house in the European Union and therefore the EU can be directed by impulses from Germany, but these impulses originate from the international ruling class and not from the people at the bottom. In Germany, the so called "rescue package" was a staggering EUR 500 billion for financial institutions (DW, 1*). Commerzbank, the second largest bank in Germany at the time, received EUR 8.2 billion in bail-out money and EUR 15 billion in debt guarantees from the Merkel government (DW, 1*). The bank then used this money from the taxpayers to take over Dresdner Bank which, as a result, ceased to exist.

Commerzbank accelerated the takeover of Dresdner Bank and was able to acquire Dresdner Bank for about half the price of an earlier bid from the Allianz group (DW, 2*). As a result of this takeover many Dresdner Bank employees lost their jobs.

This action alone caused great harm to the taxpayers. This episode was part of the transfer of assets from the bottom to the top. The money ultimately comes from the taxpayer and not out of pockets of the members of the government .

In the automobile industry small car manufacturers closed down or were taken over by larger companies. Borgward, NSU, Lloyd, AMC and more recently, Karmann and other brands have disappeared. For large corporations it is easy to outcompete small companies and arrange hostile takeovers.

The Thalidomide (also known as Contergan)

scandal is an example of the pharmaceutical industry causing unimaginable harm to babies, mothers and by extension to other members of their families. The German pharmaceutical company Gruenenthal was reluctant to acknowledge their responsibility for the damage they caused and to provide adequate financial compensation or support to the victims of this drug.

The military industrial complex is interested in developing new weapons of mass destruction. In order to ensure that there is a constant demand for these weapons, the arms manufacturers through their generous campaign contributions and overwhelming lobbying efforts, push states to create and enter into conflicts and wars.

In the UK in 2011 the estimate for the construction and production of four submarines as part of the Strategic Nuclear Deterrent was £25 billion (Mills and Dempsey*). In 2015 the costs for the same project were estimated at £31 billion (Mills and Dempsey*). These estimates were for only one project and they do not even include the maintenance expenses. This is just one example which shows that vast sums of money are involved when governments deal with arms manufacturers.

Large corporations and "not for profit" foundations provide frameworks which are ideal for psychopathic groups to carry out their ghastly activities whilst enabling them to avoid taking responsibility for their actions.

The dying society is dominated by large corporations and NGOs which serve to transfer assets and power from the bottom to the top. There are strong indications that politicians do not solve the existing problems; rather they create new problems through highly questionable actions such as the bail-outs of certain financial institutions. If there would have been a well functioning free market the poorly performing financial institutions would have failed and the competent ones would have survived. In that way a healthier financial base for the economy could have emerged.

The examples given above indicate that the dying society cannot be repaired. The ruling class obviously does not care at all about people who are not part of their small club. Too many individuals with psychopathic characteristics such as emotional illiteracy, callousness, cold-heartedness are in leading positions and they are obsessed with power.

The key issue for change is the financial system. Since the French Revolution all collapses of societies can be traced back to their unjust financial monetary systems. Even going back to ancient Rome we see the same thing. In Germany, the Weimar Republic collapsed because of extreme inflation. In the West you now have central banks which are in the hands of private investors.

In the US the Federal Reserve was created by JP Morgan. In 1913 a secret meeting took place at Jekyll Island where bankers colluded to create the Federal Reserve Bank. Despite having "Federal" in its name this bank acts in the interest of its private owners, not the general public. One may conclude that the creation of regional currencies and exchange systems (barter economy) is one of the key tasks within the emerging societies.

Under the current system, macroeconomic policy is divided into fiscal policy and monetary policy. Fiscal policy is done by the government through taxation although with BlackRock's recent "Going Direct" plan*, central banks aim to take over fiscal policy, thereby creating a situation of taxation without representation in that the central bank can simply go and take money "direct" from your account without having to go through the normal political process by which taxation is voted on and approved by elected representatives.

Monetary policy is done by the central bank through setting interest rates. Monetary policy has 3 economic objectives: full employment, price stability and economic growth, but all three of these objectives cannot be met at the same time. This means that the ruling class, through the central bank, decides which policy objectives are best for them at any point in time. For example, they have the power to crash the stock market or to create an economic boom.

There are also illegal manipulations such as the LIBOR scandal* in 2012. Several financial institutions including Deutsche Bank, Barclays, Citi Group and JP Morgan colluded to manipulate the interest rates which resulted in false interest rate calculations worldwide. Here again, the collusion of these banks served the interests of the ruling elite and was hugely disadvantageous for the majority of the global population.

How can the shift to the new system be arranged? How can the emerging fair and clean society be created? Violence cannot initiate a long-lasting positive change. The ruling class would like violent reactions from opposing individuals so that they can justify answering back with even more violence. The police forces have been equipped with military and with so called non-lethal weapons which can be lethal. Military forces are now in place which can be deployed against ordinary people.

The way of change we propose is non-violent. It follows the ideas of Mahatma Gandhi and Nelson Mandela. People like you and us who like light and fairness will find each other. Several groups have already started building communities and social structures based on our peaceful ideas. Reducing the power of the oppressive financial system can be achieved by inventing local and regional currencies or local exchange systems based on mutual trust.

We should nurture energy flows between good-natured beings. Companies in the emerging society should have their size limited and work within the circles of a nature based economy. Our companies should no longer have legal advantages over individuals. Our new economy will serve the common good. The emerging bottom up structure of regional education, economy and administration will not allow for the concentration of power in the hands of a tiny global minority.

We can finish this chapter with really good news. The emerging world we propose here is more than just a theoretical construct. The building process has already started and you can visit relevant communities which we refer to at the end of this handbook. The existence of thousands of successful initiatives demonstrates that our ideas can be and have already been implemented and work. Some of them have been active for decades, such as the Earth Charter*.

During the global crisis of the past few years many new innovative groups were created, showing that the movement is constantly growing. Currently, every day new groups are being formed. We invite you to join us!

The Old World's Leaders' Goals

In the current situation action should start at the individual level and then rise up to larger levels so that changes can be implemented at a societal level.

To understand the bigger picture with macroeconomic and political issues it helps to see and identify threats and opportunities on the individual, group and population levels. Therefore we first show below an overview of threats and opportunities of any society on the political, economic, cultural, technological, legal and environmental levels.

	Threats	Opportunities
Political	Centralised government	Decentralised structure
	One party system	Power distribution
	Rigged elections	Democracy cannot be suspended
	Corruption	
	Global organisation of political power	Clear separation of legislation, justice and government
	Tyranny	
	Dictatorship	
	Lobbyism	
	Misinformation from governments	
	The secret elite	

Economic	Large corporations	Small companies
	Economies of scale	Local currencies
	NGOs, foundations and trusts serving the ruling class	Use of cash
		No or limited use of credit cards
	Tax havens	Local banks serving the communities
	Fiat money: money without a real base	
	The debt trap	
	Profit orientation as a priority	
	War	
Society and Culture	Technocracy: - Tight regulations and digital control - Anonymity of the deep state	Traditions
		Natural healing
	Cronyism	Spirituality
		Diversity
	Use of dehumanising language: HR (Human Resources for employees)	Creating communities
		Human dimensions
		Everyone has a chance to get training
	Psychopaths and stupid individuals in leading positions	Architecture, art and music pleasing the soul
		Respecting nature
		Respecting human life and individuality

		Understanding that humans are not just an economic resource
		Real science which serves humanity
Technology	Patents in the hands of large corporations	Access to and exchange of knowledge
	Digital technology used for controlling individuals and populations	Science respecting nature
	Technocracy	Understanding that not everything should be done which can be done: ethical and moral limits
Law	Law making and judiciary in the hands of a few psychopaths and their cronies	Laws enabling a free market without the dominance of large corporations
	Tax havens	Law making by the people
	Heavy tax burden for the middle class	Protection of human rights
	Martial law	Natural law
	Laws enabling monopolies and oligarchies	Responsibility of politicians and economic leaders
	Use of psychological techniques to manipulate people	Transparency in politics and public administration

Environment		
	Large scale production of food	Small companies acting responsibly
	Profit as a main objective	Respect for nature
		Wise use of resources
	Objects made from harmful materials	No production of harmful plastics
	Single use objects which are difficult to recycle	Products with a long life span
	Little or no recycling	The production of single use products has to be justified eg, surgical items
	"Designed to fail" products	
	Long transportation ways	Recycling
		Use of natural materials
	Large corporations moving production sites to countries with no or little concern for the environment	

Let us look at some examples from the table above.

Politics

On the political front, a small group of individuals wants to establish a world government. Such a concentration of power in the hands of a very few is a recipe for destroying the diversity of human existence, freedom and democracy. If you agree, then you probably share our view that such a plan indicates a psychopathic character of the individuals behind it.

The UK is a former colonial power which has lost its position as the world's dominant super-power. The ruling class in the UK still aspires to rule the world with the help of the economic power of the US. Margaret Thatcher famously stated that the UK still has a "special relationship" with the US.

The ruling classes of other former colonial powers such as the Netherlands, Belgium, France, Portugal, Italy and Spain are also poised to join the kill.

In the US the ruling class has a long history of disregarding the lives of minorities as well as of the majority of their own population. In the 19th century, members of the ruling class were known to have had hunting parties in trains from which they could comfortably shoot and kill native Americans. In the US slaves and their descendants were often treated as sub-humans, with ethnic segregation lasting well into the 20th century.

So far the US government is the first and only government to have actually dropped atomic bombs, both in Hiroshima and Nagasaki, Japan, killing or injuring an estimated 200,000 innocent civilians in Hiroshima alone (Wellerstein*).

Various US governments have instigated dozens of wars since the second World War. President George W. Bush signed a law which protects members of the US army from being prosecuted for war crimes. Lynndie England, a member of the US army, tortured and sexually abused prisoners in Guantanamo Bay (Nbcnews*). She was put on trial, but the culprits on top of the hierarchy got away with it, as did other members of the US army who abused and tortured prisoners.

Robert McNamara*, the former Secretary of Defence from 1961 – 1968, shortly before he died in 2009 admitted that the US should not have engaged in military actions in Vietnam.

Since WW II, the US has not won a war against another country when it was the sole aggressor. Therefore a "partnership in crime" with the UK has been beneficial for achieving the inhumane goals of

32

the ruling classes in both the US and the UK (Macgregor & Docherty, 2018). Evidence for this is the Iraq War in which both the American and UK governments collaborated. Later, UN weapons inspector Blix* could not find any evidence in Iraq for prohibited weapons which were used as a justification for that war.

In the 1970s the UK government tested nuclear bombs in Australia, exposing the Aborigines to radiation. The UK government did not bother to warn the Aborigines or ask for permission to perform such tests on Australia's territory.

During the Boer War the British army committed atrocious war crimes and they were the inventor of "concentration camps" (Macgregor & Docherty, 2018).

British governments have used the strategy of divide and conquer for centuries. India was a British colony where the British government followed the strategy divide and conquer regardless of how many lives it cost.

Under Queen Elizabeth I the Crown legalised piracy as long as the pirates attacked the enemy and paid tribute to the Crown. The British government called these pirates Buccaneers. The most famous of these Buccaneers is Sir Francis Drake. Elizabeth I bestowed the title Sir to this pirate.

The three Anglo-Dutch wars are rarely mentioned. They were about securing British naval dominance. Britain was a reckless colonial power, waging wars with Sweden, France, Spain, Germany and a long list of other countries. The Crimean War of the 19th century was a war fought against czarist Russia during which Britain suffered a huge defeat. Some Russian historians call the Crimean War World War Zero because it was a huge war covering many territories. This demonstrates that the British government started wars and still continues to instigate wars in order to try to secure global dominance of its navy and to benefit the financial interests of the City of London.

Leopold II*, King of the Belgians owned the Congo as his own personal private property. He was responsible for the killing of over 10 million Africans. If the natives there did not want to work for him he had them punished by having their hands hacked off.

The First World War was arranged (Croft, 2015).

34

The German Emperor, Kaiser Wilhelm II, was a grandson of Queen Victoria and he loved England. Wilhelm II tried to avoid war (Croft, 2015). The peace treaties with Germany and Austria were deliberately unfair. In both world wars terrible war crimes were committed by both sides.

The Nazis were eager to seize power. Their party was called NSDAP, an acronym for Nationalsozialistische Deutsche Arbeiter Partei (National Socialist Workers Party). During the Nazi period Germany became a one party state. One may ask the questions: (1) Is the currently proposed world government also a one party system which pretends to act in the interest of the people? (2) Could it be that the proposed world government is acting in the interest of a few individuals of the ruling class?

Henry Ford admired Hitler and he received the highest civil order from the Third Reich. Many American companies collaborated with the Third Reich. The list of collaborating American companies includes Standard Oil (additives and petrol for the Nazi army), GM* (engines for the Nazi army), and IBM* (Hollerith computer for concentration camp administration).

Winston Churchill had a secret plan under the code name the "Operation Unthinkable"* according to which Britain would enter the war against the Soviet Union if the Third Reich could not be defeated. US General George Patton wanted to fight against the Soviet Union together with the defeated armies of the Third Reich.

There was a plot to have a fascist coup in the US in the early 1930s but US General Smedley Butler brought this plot to the attention of President Roosevelt. As a result the plot was not successful but none of the powerful and highly influential plotters was tried for treason. This is yet another example of how the law has been applied differently to different classes of society.

In the current Covid crisis fake science stated that the virus is far more dangerous than the common flu (Adam, 2020) and the unvaccinated were victims of discrimination worldwide.

The World Health Organization (WHO) has an important role in the current crisis. This organisation is not based on democratic principles. It can change the definition for a pandemic at any time and declare a pandemic without a scientific justification.

The WHO is supposedly an organisation which has the task of ensuring that health is promoted all over the world. However, the WHO's understanding of health is not a definition; it is a statement which serves the interests of large corporations (Grawath, 2022a). In addition, the WHO recommended the mRNA treatments (Covid "vaccine") but a scientific study by Fraiman et al. (2022*) shows that these treatments cause serious side effects.

The examples above indicate that the current immoral and inhumane behaviour of the ruling class reaches back in history, indicating that this type of behaviour is being handed down from one generation to the next. The dying societies have originated from these horrible actions and situations. Now more and more people are awakening to the truth that the ruling class has pursued and continues to pursue goals which are different from those professed in the public narrative.

Can any of the governments mentioned above be assumed to follow ethical and moral guidelines, or to follow fair and democratic principles?

For at least 150 years the dying societies in many

countries have deliberately been stripped by the ruling classes in many countries of any democratic and fair principles in the historic processes.

Economics

The middle class has accumulated considerable wealth and has reached a certain level of independence through self employment. Middle class professionals such as medical doctors, lawyers, tax advisors, plumbers, carpenters, tailors and others provide services or produce something.

The middle class is now under attack by global players because it is the backbone of the economy in developed economies. The middle class employs many people, produces diversity and provides professional training and education.

In Germany, for example, there is a dual system of education where students attend a professional educational institution and also receive practical training at a company, mainly in companies belonging to the middle class.

Governments have imposed tight regulations which through a large tax burden, fees and fines restrict the development of the middle class. The middle class is in competition with the large corporations, and governments have introduced laws and regulations which put the middle class at distinct disadvantages to large corporations.

The economies of scale as currently practised clearly disadvantage SMEs (Small and Medium Sized Enterprises) whilst providing huge advantages for large corporations. Governments do not tell you the truth about wars, the economy and history.

Society and Culture

The majority of people in the dying society are burdened with high compulsory payments to social security systems. The majority of working people have to pay large "contributions" into the social security systems. Administrative expenses in these social security systems are extremely high.

State pensions are prone to error and fraud (House of Commons 2022*). In the UK in 2021-22 the overpayments attributed just to fraud amounted to £6.5 billion out of a total overpayment of £8.6 billion, A shortfall of £1.46 billion in state pensions was also reported, affecting 237,000 pensioners who have suffered hardships as a result.

US public pension funds have invested in crypto-currencies* but the extent of the investments in crypto have not been fully disclosed. The current collapse of the crypto markets shows the enormous risks of these investments. According to a 2022 study, 94% of pension funds sponsored by the government and state pension funds have invested in crypto-currency (Siedle, 2022*).

The question has to be asked, "Do you trust the state pension and social benefits systems?".

Some companies have been accused of unlawfully taking money out of company pension funds such as in the case of Robert Maxwell. This case is not just a matter of poor business ethics. The Maxwell family has great influence on society and politics. Robert Maxwell's daughter Ghislaine Maxwell* was sentenced to 20 years in prison for being an accomplice in crime to Jeffrey Epstein, the criminal who arranged and documented compromising situations for politicians and other individuals in public life, and he probably kept this information in control files which could be used to blackmail the individuals who participated in these compromising situations.

Bill Clinton, former president of the US, was connected to Epstein as was his wife Hilary Clinton. Prince Andrew, the second son of Queen Elizabeth II, was stupid enough to put himself in compromising situations with under-aged women. These situations were allegedly arranged by Epstein and Ghislaine Maxwell. This was documented and used to destroy his public life and to put pressure on the British monarchy. One can only speculate about the political extent of this blackmailing operation.

Ghislaine has two sisters. Both of them are extremely rich and influential. One of them has heavily invested in the IT sector.

The Maxwell/Epstein case is just one example of individuals who are economically and politically active in a detrimental way. There are probably a few thousand individuals around the world who are responsible for the destruction of the world as we know it.

In the UK there is a strong indication that the law is applied differently according to social status. The British monarchy has several suspicious and questionable connections to paedophilia. Lord

Mountbatten, an uncle of the late Prince Philip (husband of the late Queen Elizabeth II) was a member of the British royal family (Mountbatten*). The FBI* has a file on Mountbatten where he and his wife are classified as individuals with very low morality (Mountbatten*). In this file Mountbatten is also described as a paedophile and as being very influential in society and politics (Mountbatten*).

Jimmy Savile, a television and radio professional, had friendly relationships with several members of the royal family and he was influential in society and politics (Savile 1*). Savile is alleged to have sexually abused several hundred people with victims as young as 8 years old (Savile 2*). Savile received the OBE (Order of the British Empire) and he was also knighted but the alleged sexual abuse cases span over six decades (Savile 1*). The OBE, which still exists to this day, strongly indicates that members of the ruling class continue to think in terms of the British Empire. The Guardian newspaper described Jimmy Savile as a "prodigious philanthropist" and as a close friend of Margaret Thatcher, the former Prime Minister (Savile 1*). The term "philanthropist" is also used by some of the

Western oligarchs.

One may argue that these scandals belong to the distant past but there are many more recent scandals in the ruling class.

Tony Blair took the UK to war based on the statement that Saddam Hussein had weapons of mass destruction. This was obviously not true because the winning alliance could not find a single shred of evidence for the existence of these alleged weapons of mass destructions. The lie about the weapons of mass destruction originated in the US and it shows that the governments of the UK and the US work closely together.

There was no formal investigation into this lie with legal consequences for the perpetrators, the ones responsible for starting a war with a sovereign state, to be held responsible for the deaths of many innocent people.

The general question arises whether there are two separate sets of justice, ethical and moral rules - one for the ruling class and another one for the rest of society.

In the dying societies this cognitive dissonance is not questioned by the dinosaur media or the legal system. All control mechanisms have failed. This indicates that democracy is not functioning and that governments lie extensively.

Technology

With the rapid development of expensive IT the middle class has been put at a disadvantage compared to large corporations which may have their own IT departments, can outsource IT to a separate company or both.

In some federal states in Germany small shops have to prepare their tax declarations with a PC. PCs which store customer data have to be in rooms not accessible to the customers and the entrance door has to meet certain specifications. In Malta a small shop, such as a tiny greengrocer, has to use a digital cash register which prints tax receipts for each transaction. For a large corporation such requirements do not pose a financial problem or a logistical problem but for small businesses such requirements can be an enormous burden.

Digital identity is a control instrument which is far more intrusive than any CCTV system (Closed Circuit Television). If digital identity is going to be implemented then the privacy of individuals will be completely destroyed.

A digital identity can be connected to all aspects of life including the health care system, the social system, the financial system and public administration. In fact all industries can access the digital identity which can be used to obtain information about an individual from cradle to grave. Theoretically it provides the possibility to control who is allowed to live and if allowed to live, then for how long. The questions arises: Who is going to make these decisions and what are the criteria for these decisions?

Such questions are part of the spirituality of life and cannot be taken out of the reach of the individual human being.

If AI is going to make these decisions then humanity is doomed. If some psychopaths are going to make the decisions then humanity is also lost.

A digital currency is planned in the form of a Central Bank Digital Currency and it would enable the ruling class to block access to money if an individual is not acting according to the behaviour they desire.

Using cash for payments is an effective action against the introduction of the digital currency. This is a project of the ruling class which has control over the different industries including IT, financial services, and the industrial military complex.

Law

The laws regarding intellectual property and patents favour large corporations. There are even patents on the code of life, the sequence of the DNA.

Large corporations can pay for several legal teams to represent them in court, making it very difficult, or almost impossible for small companies or private individuals to sue a large corporation.

The fees for the marketing approval of pharmaceuticals are now so high that it puts small pharmaceutical companies or individual medical doctors in the position that they cannot afford to compete with large pharmaceutical corporations.

The law has changed several times. In the 1930s in the US anti-trust laws were introduced to prevent monopolies. Vertical and horizontal monopolies are not in the interest of the majority of the population. Nowadays merges and acquisitions are used to

46

increase the size and the power of corporations.

Another danger of a monopoly is to be found in the production of food with decisions made over what is to be produced and what not. The control of the food supply provides control over the population.

Genetically modified food might have extensive dangers to the health of the population but it may increase the profits dramatically. In a food monopoly the use of herbicides and pesticides may increase further and may cause further damage to the health of the population.

Bill Gates is now the largest land owner of farm land in the US. He has also heavily invested in the production of artificially produced food, such as artificial meat and artificial baby milk.

Environment

The large chemical companies tend to avoid taking responsibility for their actions. The accidents in Bhopal, India and Seveso, Italy are just two examples of the enormous harm caused to nature and individuals by large chemical companies.

The military industrial complex has a vast array

of weapons at its disposal. There are the conventional weapons and the ABC weapons, which stands for Atomic, Biological and Chemical weapons. The ABC weapons pollute the environment, some for a short period of time and others for a very long time. Regarding humans, they do not differentiate between soldiers and civilians.

We will give you here only a few examples. Humanity seems to be of no consideration to the military industrial complex. President Eisenhower* was a general before he became president, and he warned the public about the military industrial complex when he left office in 1961. At that time three and a half million people worked in the military industrial complex and the combined net income of all US corporations was less than the US spending for the military. This shows the economic, political and social might of the military industrial complex. Eisenhower specifically warned that about the danger of the increase of misplaced power in the military industrial complex.

Depleted uranium 236 is used to make munitions deadlier (Wagner*). This type of munition was used by the American and British armies during both wars in Iraq. 300 tons of this ammunition were used in the Gulf War (Franzen, 2001). The Allies also used depleted uranium weapons in Kosovo and in Yugoslavia (Franzen, 2001). It has been calculated that the Allies used a total of 325 tons of depleted uranium in the wars in Iraq and Kuwait in 1991, in Bosnia-Herzegovina in 1995 and in Kosovo and Serbia in 1999 (Katz, 2014). In the US alone there were 500,000 metric tons of depleted uranium in storage in 1998 (Franzen, 2001).

Acidity and oxidation-reduction properties of the contaminated environment determine the contamination of drinking water with depleted uranium (Franzen, 2001).

Depleted uranium is a radioactive substance which has toxicity as a heavy metal. Bioavailability of depleted uranium has been indicated by lab experiments through simulated ingestion (Katz, 2014). The fine dust of depleted uranium is black and it is formed upon impact. Most of this black dust can be found in a circle of about 100 metres around the target hit (Katz, 2014). The fine dust can be distributed with the wind. All isotopes of depleted uranium are alpha particles which are long lived

(Katz, 2014). The decay products of depleted uranium emit alpha, beta and gamma rays (Katz, 2014). Inhalation, ingestion, subcutaneous entry (injury, accidents), and dermal contact are paths of entry for depleted uranium (Katz, 2014).

Accumulation of various doses of radioactivity occurs and there are also other sources of radioactivity. Depleted uranium can enter the food-chain since it exists in the soil in an oxidised form which is soluble and therefore it can enter the ground and surface water (IAEA*).

An anti-tank munition with depleted uranium which hits a tank can easily penetrate the armour of most tanks and inside the tank the temperature will exceed 1,000 °C. The tower is normally blown away and the soldiers in the tank are pulverised. In the case of hitting civilian targets, civilians are pulverised too.

During this process extremely fine dust is created and distributed through the explosion and carried with the wind. This toxic dust causes disease and pollutes the environment. Furthermore the toxic dust enters the body when people breathe and drink or eat contaminated food. The dust is so fine that it reaches the lung alveoles, and this makes it very hard or virtually impossible for the body to excrete this toxic dust. Wind distributes this dust over large areas, even across borders to other countries.

The Gulf War Syndrome was initially not connected to this radioactive dust but now evidence proves that this dust causes diseases such as cancer. Birth defects have been linked to depleted uranium (Wagner*), and there is also evidence that this type of munition has been used in the Bosnian wars and in Serbia. Scientific investigations also found plutonium in samples taken from these battlefields. Plutonium is the most toxic substance on earth.

Contamination with depleted uranium 236 is assumed to last for thousands of years, essentially forever. The main figures in the video *Deadly Dust* by Frieder Wagner* (2007) are Professor Dr Siegwart-Horst Günther, Professor Dr Asaf Duracovic, Dr Axel Gerdes, Dr Jenan Hassan and Tedd Weyman. This video shows that the military industrial complex does not care how much damage it causes to the environment and to civilians.

The current system provides the framework for such psychopathic activities. It is a war crime to use radioactive munitions but so far no court of law has prosecuted the people responsible for these crimes. The US government has a department of veteran affairs, and veterans who were exposed to depleted uranium and got sick from this exposure can file a claim for compensation (US Government*). Decisions about those claims are made on a case-by-case basis (US Government*). The official website *US Department of Veteran Affairs* provides only a short text about the health hazards of depleted uranium and does not provide a complete picture of the problem (US Government*).

A systematic scientific review by Surdyk et al (2021) found that 83% of the investigated studies reported positive associations between exposure to uranium and adverse health effects. The researchers use the term "weaponised uranium" because recent studies suggest that the US military also used slightly enriched uranium during the Iraq War.

Uranium can cross the placental barrier and the blood-brain barrier. Uranium can circulate through the entire body as uranyl ions. Accumulation of uranium occurs in the liver, kidney and bones.

Breaks in DNA strands are caused by an increased presence of reactive oxygen species which can be observed after uranium absorption (Surdyk et al, 2021). Local populations have a higher risk of adverse health effects compared to US veterans due to chronic exposure (Surdyk et al, 2021).

The US army used a total of more than 73 million litres of chemical weapons during the Vietnam War, of which about 45 million litres were Agent Orange (von Meding, 2017*). Agent Orange is a very potent herbicide and it also contains the toxic dioxin. The effects of Agent Orange can be handed down the generations (von Meding, 2017*). Between 2.1 and 4.8 million Vietnamese people were exposed to Agent Orange in this chemical warfare of the US army (von Meding, 2017*).

Effects of Agent Orange include various forms of cancer and serious birth defects (von Meding, 2017*).

US troops used the chemical compound napalm from 1965-72 during the Vietnam War. Napalm is a deadly weapon which incinerates its victims and causes unimaginable pain. It burns slowly at about 1,000°C (Britannica, 2022*). The US used napalm in bombs, flamethrowers and other explosives (Britannica, 2022*). Further examples of health hazards caused by chemicals and radioactive substances are described in Grawath (2022b, pp. 48-55).

The Emerging Societies' Guidelines

Based upon ethically grounded reflection and upon people who took action such as Albert Schweitzer, we formulated guidelines of the emerging society in 2015 "The Power of Vision" (Die Kraft der Vision). Several initiatives such as the Earth-Charter Movement* or the New Earth Manifesto* argue along the same lines.

The main ideas of the emerging world will be based on health, well-being and balance of all living beings on our planet. Every living being is treated with respect and mindfulness. What does that imply concretely for every human being? Let us look at some reflections formulated in the New Earth Manifesto.

We remember that we are connected to the plants and the animals on a soul level within the universal mind. We can communicate with them. The plant devas (elemental beings literally meaning "bodies of light") help us to transform our gardens and fields into energetically powerful places where vital and highly nutritious food grows. We trust the life-serving natural circles of evolution and the lightful potentials in the family of humans as well as in each of us. We celebrate variety and colourfulness instead of a standardised mash of globalised companies and their products.

Production of all things humans need will be based on a fair and circuit-oriented economy. Inspired by the "cradle-to-cradle" principle, what used to be considered "waste" becomes a "nutrient" for new production cycles. In our new economy, consumer goods are produced and bought only if they are really needed. The products are manufactured sustainably and last a long time. These products can be repaired, and all parts are recyclable. The goal of a company is no longer primarily profit, but rather the real satisfaction of customers' needs, the happiness of employees and the enduring health of the earth.

Companies are led by people who work together cooperatively, pursue the same vision and maintain a good and respectful relationship with their customers, suppliers, other partners and also with each other. They have two things in common – the joy of their work and their compassion for fellow human beings, all living beings and Mother Earth.

The production and service companies we found are small and medium-sized. They are companies which have deep roots in their respective regions. In the cities, food cooperatives and shopping groups are formed that purchase their products directly from the craftsmen and from organic farms within the region. Global discount chains and corporations are no longer needed and are therefore dissolved. They are replaced by more and more regional shops with predominantly local products.

Our economy is based on fraternity and cooperation. It serves to satisfy each other's needs. Companies see themselves as partners instead of competitors. They thrive through collaboration and cooperation.

A new financial and exchange system architecture is developed. Currency and direct exchange systems are in development or are already being developed and tested regionally. Together with regional producers, craftsmen, service providers and consumers, these will be further developed until well-functioning systems are found regionally.

Land and other public proprieties such as air or groundwater cannot belong to anyone and therefore can no longer be speculated with. The land, the air and the water are the basis of life for all living beings. The anthropocentric claim that a small minority of one amongst millions of species may determine the life base for a whole planet's life will be obsolete.

Land ownership gets a completely new definition. Land is transferred to life-supporting projects, communities or foundations. In this way, we have a fair stewardship right over a piece of land. We take responsibility for it, perceive ourselves as loving and mindful custodians of this patch of earth and protect, regenerate and care for it. Animals, plants and the organisms in the soil have just as much a natural "right" to live healthily in this place as humans.

Of course, we could continue these guidelines up to very concrete levels, i.e. the single principles of a circular economy. However, to keep track we stop here with the bird's eye perspective. You can find details in the New Earth Manifesto*, which was initiated in 2020 by Catharina Roland, an Austrian film-maker (Awake to Paradise*) and Coco Tache, a Swiss networker for the emerging society. Today the manifesto is supported by thousands of people engaging in the emerging society. Further source books for the general societal perspective are Schmuck, 2015; and for the level of founding communities the current book of Ralf Otterpohl (2022).

Human Potentials

In the course of evolution human beings have developed a number of potentials at their disposal. Potentials are components from which various things can be constructed. For example, you can make an endless number of complex figures out of some building blocks. In the case of human beings, however, these building blocks are not fixed but rather dynamic. The results are not finished buildings but fluidly balanced human beings who, at a certain point in their lives, have more or less unfolded their individual potentials.

Our potentials allow us to form our biographies as highly creative works of art. As far as we know, there is not yet a construction kit that maps the potentials of us humans in a well-sorted and reasonably complete way. For many years, as a lecturer and researcher, one of the authors has analysed the construction kits available so far in the science of psychology.

There are many proposals, but from our point of view, they almost always focus on some of the potentials and treat others only marginally or do not mention them at all. As an example, our potential for self-development or our potential for thinking and cognition were so fashionable in the second half of the last century that entire institutes and faculties at universities were devoted to them.

In principle, there is nothing wrong with that. Neglected potentials, however, may disappear from our attention. In the case of the potential to treat other living beings with respect it may happen that only a few people develop this potential. Therefore we will focus here on some of the widely neglected aspects of our functioning, namely the motivational potential and it´s relation to well-being, the emotional potential, the spiritual potential and the potential to feel at home in the flow of time.

Motivational Potential and Well-Being

Let us first have a look at a model of personality (Schmuck, 2017) including potential motivations of human beings. The motivation of humans is initially based, both from an ontogenetic and a species-historical perspective, on an ego orientation, which is an absolute prerequisite for the reproduction of the species. This orientation can be complemented by a self-transcending social orientation that includes the ego orientation. With optimal development, this orientation can also be replaced by the more comprehensive circle of biospheric orientation, which includes the social and ego orientations.

In all three orientations cognitive, emotional and

spiritual aspects can be conceptualised. This two-dimensional picture of development, modelled as concentric outward circles in the plane, becomes a sphere when another dimension is defined that runs perpendicularly through the centre of the circle. We call this dimension the time and responsibility focus.

As long as this focus is on a narrow area around the present, an individual does not consider much more than yesterday, today and tomorrow for the direction of one's life. The shape of a circle is hardly changed into the third dimension, i.e. towards a voluminous body. Even if a person takes into account the entirety of one's own (expected) lifetime for the orientation of current actions, the corresponding state of development is modelled as a flat "discus", i.e. it is still far from a potential ideal state, the spherical shape.

This potential ideal state of personality development, the spherical form, is approximated when the following processes take place: (1) a person reflects or seeks to sense in a balanced way his or her biographical roots, the roots of our species and ultimately those of all life; (2) the person understands himself or herself in his or her current life processes as part of a cosmic event which he or she helps to shape and enjoy responsibly; and finally (3) the person senses a responsibility for future life far beyond his or her own lifetime and aligns his or her own actions with it. This is in our view to date mostly neglected but in our future the most important potential when we build our society.

If you like these considerations regarding our own nature then you may agree that human beings, in general, have the potential to engage in transformation toward a socially just and ecologically thriving society. If we do that we are in line with evolution's main trajectory of unfolding growing complexity and variability. Therefore, one may expect that these persons will be rewarded with the highest gratification evolution has to offer, namely well-being.

Let us summarise. If evolution provides the outlined cognitive, emotional and spiritual development potential in us humans, then persons who develop these potentials can be expected to show a higher well-being compared to persons who only develop parts of their potential. In detail, this hypothesis is based upon two sub-hypotheses.

62

First, a growing social cohesion may be expected within the group of persons who are engaged in the common goal. Such a close social network supports well-being because being embedded in a social network results in a variety of positive experiences for the individual in his or her functioning as a social being. Further, social support may be seen as a buffer against stress.

The second sub-hypothesis for our general hypothesis of rising well-being as a consequence of unfolding our potentials is focused on the "self-efficacy" concept. Self-efficacy convictions may develop during ontogenesis when a person has opportunities to cope successfully with challenging requirements. These convictions might contribute to well-being.

And here is the good news regarding all these hypotheses. One of the authors was a researcher in psychology for 40 years and performed dozens of studies supporting the hypotheses mentioned above. Several studies by Peter Schmuck and his teams (2013) showed that people engaging in the new society experience higher well-being than others.

Emotional Potential

Let us have a closer look at our emotions. Feelings such as compassion play an important role in our everyday experiences and actions. Joy, pain, fear, a good or bad conscience - we have all felt these within ourselves. They are sensations that are extant before any thinking starts. They give us immediate feedback about the balance with our fellow world. If the balance is disturbed, negative feelings without any thinking immediately lead us to try to restore the balance through our actions.

In our culture, the view is widespread that feelings are inferior to our thinking abilities, as can be seen in pejorative terms such as "sentimentalism" or educational maxims such as "one has to avoid showing one's feelings", especially among boys. The potential to feel compassion, however, is so strongly ingrained in us that even a rather callous culture is not able to completely eliminate such feelings in most people. The emotional potential is a strong disposition of humans which is rather suppressed in our culture.

In recent years, there have been attempts to increase the value of emotions in the interplay of human potentials by psychologists developing a theory of "emotional intelligence". This neologism, however, seems rather confusing, since emotions are not a sub-area of cognitive abilities as the base for thinking and intelligent processes. Emotions are an evolutionarily older and immediate potential for regulating our balance with the world around us, which we presumably share with higher animal species.

If you have ever had close contact with horses, cats, other animals or plants in our environment, you will certainly be able to confirm this. If not, try to awake your potential emotions! Especially empathy and compassion are essential for building the society we want.

Spiritual Potential

Three reasons suggest a potential for spiritual unfoldment in human beings - not just as any one of many potentials but as a highly significant one.

(1) Many of the sharpest thinkers of the last centuries such as the physicists Albert Einstein and Werner Heisenberg have come to the conclusion that evolution is a meaningful process. Its fundamental operational principles cannot be deduced by human thinking. They concluded that we humans should therefore deal respectfully and modestly with the creation that surrounds us instead of proclaiming ourselves to be the rulers of the world and playing out all our possibilities here to make resources, animals and plants serve us.

Psychologists such as Wilfried Belschner (2007) distinguish on the personal level between an everyday consciousness in which we experience ourselves in a three-dimensional space and in a linear time sequence and, on the other hand, a holistic consciousness in which experiences of other spaces of reality become possible, for which metaphors such as God, the All-One, the Dao or the Brahman have been coined in the various cultures of humanity.

Other psychologists such as Carl Jung, Viktor Frankl (1985), Erich Fromm and Alfred Adler have modelled spirituality as a firmly anchored human psychological disposition.

(2) In all times and cultures known to us, people have exhibited behaviour that points to spiritual potential, be it shamanistic rituals or rituals of today's widespread world religions. A large proportion of the people who have lived in the time we can survey have had respect for higher powers, however they have been named. As Birgit, one of the interviewees in one of our studies (Lamprecht, 2005) puts it, *"Spiritual experience? That is being connected. Feeling connected with everything that is. Feeling one, falling out of duality. Not: there am I and there are the others. But rather: it all falls together for a moment. We are one. We belong together." "For me, the spiritual path is a way of being human. With all the love we can have, with all the compassion we can have and with the responsibility for all beings."* Or as Doris says, *"Well, I simply believe in a superordinate force that unites us all and somehow also guides us, but which I can also involve, just supporting energy, with which I am in contact, which I can tap into, so to speak."*

(3) Let us try to detach ourselves somewhat from the maelstrom of opposing arguments pro and contra spirituality and assess the issue at stake with some distance. Follow me on a little thought experiment, the result of which may seem exciting.

Arthur Köstler (1978) introduced the concept of a "holon". A holon is a whole in a more complex environment, for example a molecule, a cell, a human being, a landscape or a planet. You can pick this whole for observation and analyse it, but you will only be able to really understand each holon if you always keep two perspectives in mind - the internal perspective: each holon consists of smaller parts, which in turn can be considered as holons - and the external perspective: each holon is itself part of a larger context, a larger whole, which again can also be considered as a holon.

It is immediately clear to us in the case of *holons which are smaller than us humans*. In order to be able to understand how a cell functions, we have to understand something about the components of a cell, such as vacuoles, cell nucleus, cell wall and at even smaller levels, molecules and atoms. From an external perspective, we can only understand the

68

meaning of a cell if we are interested in the plant, animal or human body in which this cell lives and what function it has in this larger interplay. A liver cell is built differently from a nerve cell, and that has to do with the function in the larger context.

With *holons larger than us humans*, the matter also seems clear. To understand the planet Saturn, we need information about its surface and composition, but to understand its motion, we need information about the gravitational forces in the planetary system of which Saturn is a part.

And now to us humans. Every human being, in analogy to a cell or a planet, can be regarded as a holon, and if you think the last paragraphs are plausible, what applies to other holons should also apply to the comprehension of every human being. We humans can only expect success in the endeavour to comprehend ourselves if we consider the inner and the outer perspectives.

As far as the inner perspective is concerned, we have been well on the way since the Middle Ages, when the first doctors dared to open up the human body (if we disregard skull trepanations of even earlier times). In the meantime, dozens of medical disciplines have developed that deal with the different parts of our body.

When it comes to the external perspective, which should also be considered in the case of humans, as with a cell or Saturn, we are confronted with dangerous intellectual territory.

On the one hand, millions of people are pursuing the desire to understand this outside perspective. They seek to understand and influence the integration of us humans into larger contexts and processes. A few scientists have also formulated theories on this, such as Victor Frankl (1985), who assumed that the search for meaning is an original human need, the ignoring of which simply makes people ill.

On the other hand, there are broad currents in modern science that try to make us believe that spirituality - as an attempt to integrate or search for meaning in relation to larger contexts - is not necessary or even a misleading issue.

If you find our thoughts convincing and sense a potential for spiritual unfolding within yourself, the question remains, "Why are such potentials and their meaningfulness widely denied today?"

This seems to us to be connected with the hypertrophy, i.e. the pathological proliferation of the EGO and thinking potential which have developed in parallel in the past centuries. Their claim to validity left no room for spiritual events. This, in turn, could be related to the publicly not reflected power claims of social groups that profit from the current social system and are not interested in replacing it.

Feeling at Home in the Flow of Time

Most of us experience the flow of time as a line and thus our own lifetime as a section on this line. The starting point can be precisely determined at the time of birth; the end point cannot be predicted during our lifetime, but seems certain to us. This kind of experiencing time has two consequences. First, one's own lifetime will be regarded as strictly finite. Second, the feeling of being a guest on this earth arises - a guest who comes from nowhere, stays here for a fixed time, and then disappears again into nothingness.

Do we humans have the potential to escape this conviction? Can we approach a feeling of being at home in time without a fixed beginning and without a threatening end? Let us have a look at a few arguments in favour of this.

The first may seem esoteric to you, but to us it seems worth considering. The evolution of life on Earth has led to a magical diversity of life forms, to a great festival of the joy of living. Although there are processes that seem cruel to us, such as the killing of other beings for the purpose of nourishment, we are not aware of any form of life that obviously carries out its life primarily in suffering. The joy of life is one of the few facts of our existence that is difficult to doubt. Certainly all of us have experienced this feeling upon awakening on a sunny summer morning. "I am life that wants to live, in the midst of life that wants to live," summed up Albert Schweitzer one of his core insights about life.

Why should evolution create humans with novel mental capabilities and yet condemn them to lifelong agonising thoughts about the approaching end of individual existence? That would be an accident of evolution. If one believes that accidents determine evolution, one would have to put up with it and that's that.

What if one does not believe so much in accidents and concedes the possibility that evolution is not blindly experimenting? Then one can take a closer look at whether our idea of these strict time limitations of our life is appropriate.

Let us look as objectively as possible at where we come from and where we are going. Both the parts of our body and the parts of our soul experience are, strictly speaking, immortal since both are neither created out of nothing nor disappear into nothing. The parts of our body have been parts of other beings before our birth, and after our demise they will continue to be in other beings.

That which constitutes our soul life also builds on a long history of development before the time of our own birth. The person we feel ourselves to be psychologically is the product of thoughts, beliefs, messages we receive throughout our lives from other people and beings. Put more simply, our parents, teachers, siblings, friends as well as all other beings we have ever been in contact with have contributed to shape our own psyche as we perceive it today. The same applies to the time after our passing. Our own thoughts, convictions, communication habits and contents in turn form and shape other beings and thus also do not disappear into nothingness but live on in other contexts.

What actually has a beginning and an end are the ego-parts in the human being and the special unique combination of physical and psychic characteristics that come together in a person. The "I" really dies, which is why it makes so much sense to transcend the "I". That is the ultimate goal of some spiritual traditions such as Buddhism, leading to enlightened souls feeling themselves as parts of the universal mind.

Are there individuals who do not experience themselves as strangers or guests on a timeline? Are there individuals who perceive themselves quite naturally as a link in a chain of meaningful events who therefore do not associate any painful thoughts or feelings with the limitation of life time? Are there individuals who have developed the potential for integration in time, as we would like to put it?

Yes, they do exist. Since the Middle Ages craftsmen and farmers handed down businesses that they took over from their parents and passed on to their descendants in a well-kept condition. Even today it is a matter of course in many families that parents pass on the best they can give to their descendants or to other people. This seems to be an expression of the fact that people experience this involvement; otherwise one would not have to worry about the living conditions of future generations.

A particular example of this is one of the authors' ancestors named Joseph Benedict Polednik. His only son, for whom the handover of his life's work was intended, died at the age of 18. What did Mr Polednik do? He put his financial resources into a charitable foundation that provided education and care to disadvantaged people for many generations.

If you are looking for people who are engaged in future issues today, you can easily find many examples. This, too, we consider an important argument in the search for evidence that we humans have the potential to be involved in time.

People are presumably capable of reflecting on the past and possible future developments in order to draw conclusions for a meaningful life of their own in the chain of generations. And a person who has developed this potential will be able to act, feel and enjoy a large part of his life time in the here and now.

This person perceives and feels the integration into time described here and can draw strength and direction for meaningful, good actions from it.

Second Step: The Options

The descriptions and analyses of our book's diagnosis part may help you to identify the dark forces which you encounter in the dying society. On the other hand, looking at the emerging societies' guidelines and our potentials to follow these lines you might be well prepared to detect lightful opportunities for yourself and a new, fair society. You can use these options to improve your well-being as well as to the advantage of the future world.

Two aspects seem to be crucial in searching for your place in the emerging society.

A top-down question sheds light on the points of origin of the new society. Which activities are required at particular places in the cities and villages of our new world?

A bottom-up question complements the emerging figure with considerations of your role. What might be your specific contributions on some of the points of origin?

Where Are the Points of Origin?

The potential points of origin for our emerging lightful, fair and balanced world span all aspects of society we described above. Politics, economics, culture, technology, law and environment are the main fields which may be divided into more differentiated aspects respectively.

Looking at culture, for instance, we find schools which support the unfolding of creativity, the enjoyment of life and the empathy among our children. We find universities which perform science and education serving humanity and respecting the creation we are embedded in. There are medical centres based upon natural healing traditions and there are musical activities bringing us in resonance with the universal mind. Alternative architecture creates human scale buildings constructed from regional building material with open source DIY instructions.

This book is not the place for a differentiated analysis of all these fields. We want to encourage you to start with concrete actions in the region where you live. Therefore we give some examples of points of origin which are the base of the future society.

The foundation of a sane society are regions, villages or communities where people produce healthy food, fertile soil, clean air and clean water, and care for biodiversity. In these communities all aspects of life are included in a nutshell. An advantage of this concrete approach may be that you can start tomorrow to look around in your region for where   attractive options are for you.

Ralf   Otterpohl,   a   German   scientist   and practitioner, proposes new villages following the guidelines of the emerging society (2017, 2022). These emerging villages and regions are sustainable alternatives to the rural exodus and urban overpopulation. A community size of 150-300 inhabitants, he says, would be suitable for building an infrastructure on a basis of personal trust.

Instead of an agricultural desert of monocultures, edible paradises are created within the community. Instead of huge machines compacting the soil for generations, many people are finding meaningful work again. The farmers can save their farms for the future with management which considers the rules of nature. The townspeople receive, for example through the organization of community supported agriculture* teams, a variety of fresh regional food.

The emerging communities may be organised as cooperatives leasing or buying the land from the owners. People from neighbouring towns can also connect with the emerging communities through cooperative shares.

The new communities may consist of many small or even tiny farms. An existing farm can be transformed into a "mother farm" that becomes a community and logistics hub. Instead of a farming family working 7 days at the subsistence level, a so-called garden village offers many "mini farmers" on their plots a sufficient income in the future in addition to achieving self-sufficiency. The recommended size per farm is about one hectare for one family.

A group of about 150 people corresponds to the ancient clan size. Up to 300 people may still know each other at least by sight. This is one precondition for mutual trust. The village should not get any bigger. The basic open concept of a "New Village" or garden village should create an interesting social environment.

The aim is for children to find their peers, for young people to find their partners and for older people to find home care options just in case. Due to the size of around 150 people, a number of other small businesses can be created in addition to horticulture, as well as a local service sector. If a suitable environment is already in place, the same advantages can of course also arise with smaller projects. With the self-responsible garden plots, there are even more neighbourly structures than in a nearby community.

It appeals to individuals with a focus on the meaning of life, the desire to do something for the community and society and to live in nature. In the new village, people with great experience can make many important contributions. Intergenerational living in the new village is a good option.

Mini-farmers are micro-entrepreneurs who are also active in areas such as crafts, marketing, social events, administrative work, art, culture, education and therapeutic tasks.

Regarding the core business of the mini-farms, organic vegetable cultivation, its marketing and sales are organised within a cooperative.

The top priority is the revitalisation of humus in order to create fertile soil and preserve it for the future. Humus-rich soil holds water and regenerates groundwater, prevents drought and flooding, and produces more and better food. Instead of expensive and energy-consuming waste water systems, dry toilets are used which return the organic waste materials to the fertility cycle by using the Terra Preta process with the addition of activated carbon.

The independent production of seeds, crop diversity and experience with ideal crop neighbours are particularly important. "Edible" tree seeds such as chestnuts and walnuts provide food with the highest quality.

The diverse small areas with permaculture/bio-intensive cultivation and agroforestry systems increase the diversity of species and enlarge the vital humus layer. There are scientifically supported examples that prove that permaculture* can bring

82

very high yields.

The surplus can be processed and marketed directly on site or in the cities. In the long term, the cities can be supplied by garden villages in the vicinity through garden rings. These garden rings or garden regions can arise when there are several new villages around a city. Then there can be specialisations in production, joint purchasing and an exchange of goods and ideas.

Mini-farmers live with a small footprint on their mini-farm in ecological mini-houses or modular houses. Living together with plants and animals in one's own horticultural business is crucial for the success of the mini-farms. By using common areas, individual space requirements can be significantly reduced. A greenhouse can also be used as an extended living space (earthship*).

The concept of flexible mini-houses offers a way to adapt organically to the garden landscape. They are relatively inexpensive and can be set up by a small group of people within a short time. There are already some kits of prototypes for tiny houses (Wohnwagon* and Arched Cabins*). Modular homes may be adapted to the family circumstances.

The essential goal of the new village should be the good life as a creative part of an increasingly diverse and productive nature. Therefore, a beautiful environment is an important factor. In the new village there should be a relaxed life with exercise, personal development through contact and interaction with nature. A varied life with physical activities in the sun and food straight from the field are already a good prerequisite for health. A positive attitude to life, creative opportunities and contact with interesting people keep us fit.

There are holistic methods that can, for example, drain heavy metals and dissolve blockages of all kinds in order to become healthy and happy and to stay healthy into old age. For details look at Ralf Otterpohls platform Garden Ring Cities* or one of his books about new villages concepts (2017, 2022).

My Specific Potentials

How can you find out where you can contribute to building the new society? Four questions might support you in finding a good answer: (1) What have I really enjoyed doing in my life so far? (2) Are there any activities that I have never done but that I would really enjoy? (3) What are the unique challenges and needs of my family, community, region, country, or planet and which activities are necessary now? (4) Where is the overlap between what I am good at and enjoy doing on the one hand and what the world around me needs right now?

Different people like different activities. Some like to teach a subject, others get joy from constructing or repairing mechanical tools, instruments or machines. Some are happy to produce food such as cheese, wine, beer and enjoy growing biological fruits and vegetables. Others experience flow when they learn languages, play music or create computer programmes. There are people who manage projects, create platforms and provide advice to others with great fulfilment.

You may continue this list by looking at the passions of your friends and parents, of your four grandparents and of your eight great-grandparents. Then, look at your own past experiences. Start with your earliest memories. Check these experiences for the inner fulfilment you felt doing these actions. Then you can realise what your potentials are. Be aware that what you have done up to this day is only a small percent of the potential dormant within you. Look at biographies of older people and ask the most interesting among them about changes in their life priorities and activity patterns. We know some people who started new professions and hobbies at the age of 70 and over. The grandmother of a friend started skydiving as an 80 years old woman, to give an example.

Now let us look at the specific demands in your vicinity. Are there demands for practical skills such as repairing bicycles or for harvesting and processing fallen fruits? Are there older people who need support in housework and shopping? Are there people who would enjoy learning from you how to handle modern IT devices? Are there younger children who would be happy if you would share your time and experience with them? Do you know disabled people who are in need of support in integrating our abilities? Do you know who in your neighbourhood is lonely, desperate or simply often sad?

After doing that analysis for a while you will have a long to-do list indicating the challenges in your circle of observation. Probably the list is too long for your available time and energy.

After reflecting thoroughly upon the first three questions you will then be in a comfortable situation to answer the last question, "Where is the overlap between my preferences and potentials and the needs of the actual world around me?"

Working on projects for fair world teams needs members who complement each other in terms of abilities. Therefore you may be confident that you will find a proper place in the emerging communities around you. We invite you to have a closer look at this challenge in the next chapter.

In a few cases it may be that your actual main passion is not in the top places of the to-do list in your community. If you are a passionate philosopher or an instrument maker for zithers you might find out that your group is not highly interested in integrating you. Then you have two choices. You can move to a group which is in need of your specific ability, or you can consider to perform your passion part-time and you try if some of the urgent activities of the group's to-do list are fulfilling for you.

Third Step: My Specific Activities

Now let us focus on your very personal/individual contributions for initiating and supporting the blossoming process of our lightful and fair communities. Here we invite you to reflect on which way you can find or form a substantial group of people which is based on mutual trust. Such groups are like embryonic cells of the new society, creating and completing the new life forms we have in mind.

Once you have a group of people, the next challenge is to find your proper place in that organism. This depends on your own process of integrating in the spiritual universe on the one hand. On the other hand you have to find out what the appropriate overlap is between your individual potentials and the actual needs of the group. What activities are needed by the emerging community and can be offered by you? Reversely formulated, which of your strengths are needed by the emerging community?

Finding the Right People

Humans are social beings. Our well-being depends on social support within groups of like-minded people. Therefore, our success in building a fair, clean and lightful society requires that we build strong groups. That is, indeed, a key function of a light ambassador - to find the right people, to motivate and to support them for cooperating in our big endeavour.

First let us have a look at the options. You might consider convincing your friends, relatives and work colleagues as well as former colleagues to join our wonderful idea.

If you tried it, you possibly share our experience with this option. In some cases this may work. But some of your former friends, kind colleagues and relatives may be strongly connected to the old world. Being employed and receiving income in the dying society may be perceived by such people as a financial dependency. The individual often feels that there is no choice other than staying at their current place, regardless of whether the employer is a university, a large corporation or a public administration entity. Some individuals simply decline any communication about the issue in order to avoid dissonance.

We are now prepared to look around ourselves for people who are open to be companions in creating the emerging society. Searching for them within the general population, let's say in a supermarket, does not seem to be very promising. There we will find a colourful mixture of people regarding our search filter. Many of them will be obedient followers of the old system or even its masterminds and profiteers. Discussions with casual acquaintances can waste valuable energy unless you feel resonance with them on a spiritual level we described above.

A better way we prefer to seek out personal contacts with people sharing our vision of the emerging society is by using the snowball principle within our growing network of new friends.

After finding a core group of people you trust one of the next challenges is to select newcomers. As you know, one rotten apple may spoil the whole barrel. We recommend intensifying common actions with newcomers to your network only after you have established a personal relationship. Only through personal contact will you find out whether you can trust a particular person. Mutual sympathy is important, but also check if your potential friend or partner has a biography that aligns with his or her current views and goals.

Of course you may meet people who maintain that they just decided to change from positions within the dying society to our communities. In such cases be careful and check in a slow step by step approach during your cooperation whether this person is worthy of your trust. You should know at this point that the dying society pays people to infiltrate and disturb any attempts to create alternatives we are working on.

Let us summarise this paragraph: Networking is essential in forming groups able to create our fair world. Be careful regarding your partners. Make sure that there are no spies or traitors among them.

My Place in the Universe

Each human individual is part of a family, of a regional group of people, of a nation, of the world population, of the biosphere of our planet and even of the universe. First time we reflect about embedding ourselves within these circles of different levels our place in these different contexts seems to be fixed.

Mature individuals, however, find more and more degrees of freedom in changing their own position or in fixing a new direction toward a completely alternative position in our future. Two examples may illustrate what is meant.

Followers of a certain religion, let us say Christians, may one day find out that there have been criminals or psychopaths among the leaders of their religious institutions. They may stop visiting Christian places of worship or seek to convert to another religion.

Employees of a prestigious company may find out that the traditional portfolio of high quality products for the consumer market has been enlarged by products for military purposes. These people often leave that company because of an inner conflict of conscience.

All of us are able to decide such changes. In every moment of our lives each of us is able to decide to stop or continue the former way of life. Let us look for details.

Inner World: Spirituality

The world of tomorrow will be the world that we humans living today intend to have. If we all agree that we want to spend our lifetime completely in artificially created environments, tomorrow's world will become reality in this form.

What would happen if individuals today, you and us, agree that we will develop more suitable patterns of life which are more attractive than those of the recent past? What would happen if we trust the positive power of the universal spiritual mind? We might bring these patterns of life to reality. By doing so we support the birth of a luminous world.

And here is some really good news. Almost every day over the past few years, we have met people who not only carry new ideas around in their heads but also simply implement these ideas very concretely on site! Some of our students started companies and organisations that produce good local food (Jonas Lackmann*) or clean energy (Michael König*). Other friends have established new schools (Bianca Höltje*) and educational institutions (Daniele Ganser*). They have built houses from natural building materials (Claudius Kern*). They have tackled the recovery of our farmland (Franz Keiser*). They have created biotopes and natural gardens, bred old varieties of fruit and preserved biodiversity (Thomas Penndorf*).

We have asked many of them in dozens of studies where they get the energy to build the emerging world. Many have told us that they believe in a deep and positive power of evolution, creating the miraculous variety of creation early humans found on our earth.

How can you tackle it very concretely - bringing your life, thinking and feeling in harmony with the universal mind?

Fortunately, the paths to the universal mind are not a secret. They are widely known and you will surely be able to find people easily in your circle of acquaintances or in your region who will help you, who will support you if you want to follow this path or want to deepen it further. How can you locate them?

How can you recognise people who have already progressed a bit along the way to the universal mind? They are people who move mindfully in the here and now. If you are walking in a crowd, you only need to look around for which people radiate calm, are friendly, perceive other people and beings, who greet you, give you a friendly nod or smell a flower by the wayside, who take the time to look at the clouds or at the treetops.

Just talk to people like that. Tell them that you are curious about how they have learned to be open to the things and beings of their world in the here and now. If you do not dare simply to speak to strangers then first look among your family and friends for such mindful behaviour. Or just behave like this yourself.

On the way to school, pay close attention to puddles, insects, clouds, people, snow crystals, birds, things with a soul as well as things that appear to have no soul. Then it will happen to you at some point that other people will notice you and start talking to you. What sparks between you when you find each other and enter into an exchange can be called resonance. In such moments you feel a vibration, a positive energy that you share. And that is already a first inkling of sensing the universal mind.

The other day, while walking, one of us met a young woman with three children who were about one year old. After the woman had lifted the children out of a wagon and put them on the forest path we greeted each other. Two children trotted off; the third one looked at me. The child didn't know me. I crouched down and we looked at each other curiously for a while. After I chatted a bit and apparently had amused the child with gestures and jumping, the child, in tune with himself and the world, happily ran off. Such an exchange with special people in your environment is a way to feel the universal mind more precisely.

Another way is one of the countless types of meditation. You have probably seen people in parks making slow, mostly beautiful movements on the spot and seeming to sink into themselves or into the world. If you ask them what they are doing they will tell you about Yoga, Tai Chi, Falun Gong or similar practices.

What all such exercises and processes have in common is that the practitioners practice mindfulness alone or in groups. Mindfulness for what? It is about feeling the magic of creation that surrounds us every moment of our lives and also fills our inner being. "And why should one practice that?" you might ask yourself at this point.

Observe for yourself what is going on in your head and your body between waking up in the morning and falling asleep in the evening. Many people are almost continuously involved in the many never-ending moments of waking consciousness in a soliloquy of their own thinking with themselves.

What's to do today? Have I checked off all my tasks for today? How will I survive maths class? How much time is left until the homework has to be handed in? What will I do this afternoon if the bus doesn't come on time again and I miss the connection? Will my dad get well soon? It's my girlfriend's birthday next week. What can I do to make her happy? What am I going to do tonight if Mummy and my brother are fighting again?

If this sounds familiar to you, you may have experienced the result. You run from home to school, from there to a friend, to the market and back home again, with your head down and deep in such thoughts. In such periods you are not centred, not in the here and now. You do not notice what enchanting cloud formations are passing above you. You do not notice the light playing on the foliage or on the snowflakes, the squirrels playing on big gnarled logs in the park. You do not notice whether other children or human-beings are suffering or happy. You are cut off from life, from the soul of the world, and you feel alone in your misery and sad thoughts.

Thousands of years ago, people on all continents invented different types of meditation to escape suffering of this kind. Since then, meditation has been practised in countless places around the world. The practitioners see the goal of all meditation in the fact that we humans deliberately practice interrupting the soliloquy of our thinking so that we initially timidly and occasionally - and later more frequently, perhaps even permanently - learn to perceive directly the magic of creation in our environment and in ourselves.

In this process, the conviction of a stable ME, which has to fight for its survival and well-being in a sometimes hostile world, dissolves. In place of this ego without connection to the universal mind there is the wonderful image of a soul that swims in the current of the universal mind and which feels invited to sense its own destiny and to express it in the flow of the great stream of events for the benefit of all beings.

If you start to get interested in meditative exercises, you will quickly realise that there are almost endless variations of meditation with scores of different names: autogenic training, breathing meditation, transcendental meditation, physical exercises such as Hatha Yoga or Sivananda Yoga.

You do not need to know every one. There is no single meditation technique that works equally well for everyone. It is enough if you pay attention to people who seem closer to the goal of each meditation than you currently feel. And these people will reach out to you for possible steps in your life. They will advance you on your way.

One can even invent one's own meditation from

the suggestions of others. On a visit to a sacred place of the Esselen Indians on the Pacific coast, I began to breathe with trees. You probably know that trees, like us humans when we breathe, absorb gases and release them again. Now the exciting thing is that a gas that we breathe out (carbon dioxide) is required by the trees to "breathe in". And vice versa. Trees give off a gas that we humans urgently need when we breathe in. Which gas? Yes, it is oxygen. So since that time, whenever I want to step into the here and now, I stand against a tree, lean my chest and arms against it, close my eyes and breathe slowly. I breathe in… and breathe out…

Then I imagine the tree breathing at the same time as me. I change my focus to the tree. I sense the same event happening from the tree. My exhalation is its inhalation and vice versa.

After a while I change the perspective again. Now I imagine that I perceive what is happening from a point outside of man and tree, perhaps from the perspective of the universal mind. Then what remains is only the movement of a gas mixture that is exchanged between two beings for their mutual benefit. If I practice this for a while, I become in the here and now with all the fibres of body and mind - mindful, grateful, humble and happy. The merry-go-round of thoughts described above stands still. If this has made you curious, give it a try.

The effects of meditation on our soul are summarised in Klische (2006). He reports an increase in our aliveness, our compassion, our ability to think, our positive feelings of well-being, our joyful vibrations and our intuition. Our life becomes more intense. We perceive more things than before. A third eye opens, so to speak, which sweeps away the veils of the past and leads us into a flood of light, into enthusiasm and high creativity in the certainty of the existence of a divine power.

Let us summarise: The common goal of the spiritual traditions of mankind consists of using techniques like meditation to become aware of the obstacles to a clear perception of the world and the universal mind. After being aware of these obstacles as the "I"-centred permanent distortion of perception, these veils may be removed.

The result of this process is called differently in different traditions, such as ENLIGHTENMENT, NIRVANA or SATORI.

Material World: Joyful Activities

Due to the crumbling trust in the classic players of the old social structures in Germany as well as in many other countries, there are currently emerging new regional communities. In such communities trust between people who know each other personally is the base for all ongoing activities. Therefore we propose to call such groups of people "Trust Communities". Other terms in use are "Cultural Oases", "Future Communities", "Solidarity Communities", "Gallian Villages" or "HELFA Communities".

To inspire you to find effective and joyful ways to contribute to the emerging society we will tell you success stories about people who found each other and together started building such communities. Enjoy some examples for several areas for which solutions were found on different points of origin of the emerging society!

What matters when we build communities based on regional trust? You will find below some topics relevant for our every day life, starting with food. Each of the points is illustrated by one or more

102

practical success stories. We finish the chapter with some overarching projects worldwide in which several aspects of the transformation are addressed.

Food

Food is essential for our life. Therefore let us start with this topic. What can you do in this field? You can contact farmers or gardeners in your region. Story one tells you about cooperatives, in which people like you got together with local farmers to produce jointly high quality food. Story two tells about people reclaiming land area in their region and cultivating this land.

(1) It is well known that a healthy body and a healthy immune system need high quality food. Slowly but surely the majority of people will learn that healthy food does not come from industrialised agriculture based on agrochemicals, genetically modified organisms, artificial insemination and GPS-controlled harvesting robots.

And so a new trend is spreading in communities all over the world. Community Supported Agriculture* (CSA) is the name given to communities in English-speaking countries that are striving for a new food supply. There are already over 1,700 CSA organisations in North America. In German-speaking countries 284 communities have been founded during the past decade, which practice "Solidarische Landwirtschaft" (SoLaWi*) which means "agriculture based on solidarity".

The basic idea is that farmers or gardeners join forces with people in the surrounding towns. City dwellers pay farmers fixed amounts in advance, and in many cases they also support the work in the countryside. Fresh food is then delivered from the countryside to the townspeople using short distances. The local people in the new CSA or SoLaWi associations decide which foods are produced and by which methods. The 2020 crisis led to a skyrocketing increase in interest in local food. An additional option is to collect money and to pay off the farmer's bank credits and debts in exchange for good food in the coming years.

If you are lucky enough to find out that one of the 284 SoLaWi companies in Central Europe or one of the 1,700 CSA operations in other parts of the world is near your home region, you can join and start tomorrow. Otherwise you can consider setting up such an organisation in your region.

(2) The Association for the Promotion of Organic Farming and Landscape Conservation in the German village Reetz* demonstrates how to counter industrial agriculture in the fields of our villages with ecological use of the landscape in the hands of the citizens. For this purpose, the association has acquired 20 hectares of farmland on the outskirts of the village, which can feed 100 people. Another focus is landscape maintenance. That means restoring and maintaining typical natural biotopes.

According to the principle of "arable land in consumer hands", the association invites people to finance the land with their membership. The benefit is an environmentally friendly, ecological production method. With the interest-free member loans, the interest-bearing purchase credit is replaced so that the project is secure for the future.

Heat

(1) The use of renewable raw materials instead of fossil resources is a forward-looking alternative for generating electricity and heat. In 2007 the citizens of Oberrosphe* in Germany started to supply the

village with green energy. For this purpose, a commercial goods and services cooperative was founded in that year.

Construction work began in Spring 2008. During a construction period of 6 months, a 7,000 metre long, new local heating network was laid and a biomass heating plant was set up on the outskirts.

Since October 2008 the biomass heating plant using wood has been in operation. In order to generate electricity, a photovoltaic system with a maximum output of 77 kW was installed in an area of 1,300 square metres and it has been connected to the grid since December 2008.

The inhabitants of the village are no longer dependent on imports of fossil fuels. 200 further villages in Germany have been inspired by our teams to produce electricity and heating energy on the basis of locally available resources (renewable energy villages*).

(2) Another option is to heat houses with solar energy. The company Fasa AG* in Chemnitz, Germany has been building such houses and heating systems for years. Even entire villages now rely on the combination of solar energy and wood for

their "village central heating".

Currently eight villages in Germany are demonstrating how this can be done (solar heating villages*). During winter, the heating network is supplied with heat from wood combustion and in summer primarily by a large solar thermal system on the outskirts. These places get about 20% of the energy they need from the sun, 80% from wood. Experts expect that the solar share can be increased by larger solar thermal fields and storages. In Dronninglund*, Denmark, a city with 3,000 inhabitants, 50% of the heat requirement is covered by solar heat.

Electricity

There are many ways to produce and distribute electricity in your region without imported fuels and without the big power grid. There are pioneers in exploiting regional sources and founding regional plants, in building own power grids, in constructing DIY solar islands or small wind turbines.

(1) Mayor Hans-Jörg Birner from the future community of Kirchanschöring* initiated the founding of a regional plant based on renewable

energy sources which will supply the 16 member municipalities with renewable electricity and heat.

(2) The 49 houses of the small village Feldheim* near Berlin are supplied with locally generated heat and electricity. For the inhabitants of Feldheim, energy self-sufficiency means not only using the heat from a biogas plant which is operated by the local agricultural cooperative. In addition to the local heating network, a separate electricity network was also installed in Feldheim. The people in Feldheim obtain their electricity directly from a wind farm through their own network, independently of the public power grid. The villagers get their electricity at an advantageous price that is well below the regular market price.

(3) Did you know that it is easy to create a crisis-proof solar island*? It takes a day to connect a few PV panels via a solar controller and an inverter with two accumulators to form a 220 volt PV island. We learned about this from Andreas Klawitter, a Thuringian friend and new world activist. In 2020 he showed us how to assemble the components for such islands. Meanwhile our island works perfectly and we use it happily for solar music, for solar

massages, for solar-mixed smoothies and e-bike tours with solar-charged batteries. In the event of a power failure we are prepared to supply heating controls and pumps with our electricity. It is so easy to create a feeling of security!

(4) During Pentecost 2019, a wind turbine with wings of 2 meters in diameter was built in Cobstädt, Germany during a DIY workshop organised by Thomas Penndorf, the local initiator of the community, Jonathan Schreiber, the workshop manager with many years of experience in small wind turbine construction and one of the authors. The DIY windmill with wooden wings supplies 1,000 kWh per year. That is exactly the average electricity demand of one person in Central Europe.

In 2022, for the 4th year in a row, there was another wind turbine workshop at the Lebensgut Cobstädt*. Meanwhile visitors to Cobstädt may admire a DIY community wind park there!

Communication

Do you know that it is possible to build local communication networks without electromagnetic radiation which are called LiFi* and which can replace WiFi? If not, enjoy the following success story.

About 10 years ago, Dr. Suat Topsu, professor of theoretical physics at the University of Paris Sanclay, developed within a few days a data transmission system for his house based on the light from LED lamps. Why? His wife had asked him to turn off wireless communication via WiFi at home during her pregnancy.

Prof. Topsu called his process "Visible Light Communication" (VLC technology), i.e. visual light communication. Prof. Harald Haas from the University of Edinburgh gave the process the elegant name LiFi in 2011 - an analogy to WiFi.

The Fraunhofer Heinrich Hertz Institute in Berlin developed this technology further. In June 2013 project manager Anagnostis Paraskevopoulos presented the VLC technology to medical doctors and ministry representatives in Baden-Württemberg. The state government then financed a pilot project on the island of Mainau. The city administration of Stuttgart financed a project in a local school. Both projects were technically successfully completed and contributed to the implementation of the technology.

Today you can buy VLC technology. It is now in use in the press centre at the Hamburg football club.

There are also hospitals in which the electromagnetic radiation associated with standard wireless networks is considered questionable because of detrimental effects on health. The regional hospital in Perpignan*, France checked the electromagnetic emissions on site and every single device was within the proposed limits. However, the combined values of all WiFi-based devices exceeded the recommended exposure limit for electromagnetic radiation many times.

This is why this clinic in Perpignan in southern France has been equipped with LiFi transmitters since 2014. The pregnant women of the Perpignan region queue up to give birth to their babies at this clinic instead of others using WiFi. Further research is needed to assess the health outcomes of LiFi technology.

Education/Care of Children

New learning environments are under construction in many countries where our children can unfold their potentials needed for our emerging society.

(1) Ricardo Leppe was lucky enough to grow up very differently from the majority of children in our part of the world. As a child, he almost never got to know any regular school from the inside. Instead, he learned mainly outside of traditional schools from adults in his area and he received a completely different upbringing and diet than is usual. After graduating from high school, he started his own business as a magician. Some time later he became active as a memory trainer. In this field he has now inspired more than 100,000 people in his lectures. Today, through his activities, he has established a learning culture that follows the slogan "Learning can, may and should be fun".

More than 100 Ricardo Leppe* open source learning courses can be called up on the internet free of charge.

(2) The Knittlingerhof* training workshop in Austria, located between Salzburg and Passau, has been working for 30 years according to the following concept:

We are convinced that every person has the full potential and can carry out all the development and learning processes that are necessary for self-

realisation in an appropriate environment. We want to respect the form, timing and duration of each child's developmental steps and not direct them through influence and manipulation in ways that would suit our own ideas.

We trust that every child chooses when which steps are important for their growth and for the fulfilment of their life plan - as long as they find the necessary living conditions. We therefore strive to create these conditions in the form of a relaxed atmosphere, respectful relationships and a prepared environment. In our school there are no exams and no grading, but all children of different age groups learn together according to their own rhythms and their own inner structures.

More than 70 pupils and 17 kindergarten children are currently being accompanied by a total of 8 carers.

(3) Some young people from the Vogtland Region in Germany recently initiated the Herzkraftwerk endowment* which supports holistic educational work. It enables children to learn with and from each other, to achieve individual educational goals, and to develop and grow in a

social context. Learning again takes place in a playful, true-to-life, close-to-nature and contact way, accompanied by mentors and specialists.

The vision of the initiators includes the creation and design of natural learning places with the aim of enabling learning while living, integrating closeness to nature, sport, culture, art, music and much more and aiding young people to have a responsible life.

Transport

The emerging society has to replace finite raw materials like fossil resources with renewable raw materials. Regarding fuel for transport the question is, "How may motorised transport based on petrol, diesel or fossil gas be overcome?". Let us look at two approaches.

(1) Delivering packages without emissions? This can work quite simply by setting up an environmentally friendly and fair bicycle courier service. This is what happened in Leipzig, Germany in 2016: Christina Kleinau was just doing her doctorate at Leipzig University in the subject of business ethics. In a circle of friends with Sandra Tappendorf and Petros Petrezikis, Christina came

114

up with the idea of the courier service. Since then several hundred emission-free courier journeys are made every day in Dresden, Leipzig and Hannover, and a nationwide bicycle courier service* provides sustainable logistics services. Unique so far in Germany! It is great that there are pioneers like Christina, Sandra and Petros! Is this an idea for you?

(2) In Schleswig-Holstein there are currently around 20 public filling stations* offering bio-CNG (compressed natural biogas). This fuel is produced completely from renewable raw materials such as biomass, and the fuel can be used for agricultural traffic machines as well as commercial and construction vehicles with CNG engines.

House Building

Do you agree that regionally available building materials for our houses such as for instance wood, straw and clay are healthier than chemical products like styrofoam as insulation material or floors based on PVC (polyvenylchloride)? Do you agree, that collecting water and generating electricity and heat on site is smarter than becoming dependent on large suppliers? Our examples provide you with options how to start building your own house.

(1) Mini-houses in all imaginable shapes are becoming increasingly popular because they prove that you can have a piece of heaven even with little money and space. The provider of Arched Cabins* has committed itself to exactly this goal. The smallest hut is available for around €900. On request, each of the houses can be equipped with countless extras, such as a fireplace, different foundations and they come in all colours.

Before you order a kit sent from Texas, Joshua Cruey, the inventor of this product series, encourages us to do it ourselves. He says,

"I started our website development and marketing in 2013/2014 and have continued my efforts as the demand for Arched Cabins has steadily increased. In 2022 my family includes my fiancee Rachael and our 5 children aged 6 to 16 years. I have been involved in fabrication and design for 25 years and have personally led building teams from a hands-on perspective for over 100 bow huts. During my years building Arched Cabins (2014-2020) I have continually refined the process to make it easier for our customers to build their

own Arched Cabin."

(2) "Building healthy. Conserving resources. Living consciously." These are the guidelines of the company Lorenzsysteme* in Taucha, Germany offering construction elements for houses made of wood and straw which are superior to conventional building materials in terms of building physics parameters. The elements can be installed easily, quickly and cleanly as exterior or interior walls. They meet the legal requirements for fire protection and insulation and do not require the use of chemicals or harmful substances during production, assembly or use.

The elements are open to diffusion and create a healthy, pleasant climate in living and working spaces. At the end of the product life the elements can be completely composted after dismantling.

(3) In addition to the advantages of the first examples, tiny houses offer independence from the usual supply lines. Electricity, water and heat are generated on site. How does it work? For example through photovoltaic off-grid systems with large storage, solar and wood central heating systems for heat and hot water supply, organic toilets (dry

separation toilets with Terra Preta bedding) or water circulation systems with green sewage treatment plants. The company Wohnwagon* builds such self-sufficient systems and they are already in use in Central Europe. If you are curious how that works in practice, guided tours, even trial living may be arranged in Vienna.

(4) In London two architects offer open-source construction kits for simple, cheap, and energy-saving houses. Their shared knowledge platform WikiHouse* makes it easier for everyone to design, craft and assemble modern houses tailored to one's own individual needs.

Repairs

The dying system is a throw-away society. Therefore repairing everyday items is not a key issue in the old world. If we want to overcome that we need a repair culture. Keep in mind, all group activities such as repairing items in circles of like-minded people sharing substantial visions and values serve your well-being (Schmuck & Sheldon, 2001)!

(1) At more than 1,500 locations in Germany, volunteers organise repair cafés* where broken

118

everyday items are repaired together in a relaxed atmosphere. Such activities may support waste avoidance as well as resource and environmental protection. Additionally, they enable neighbourly networking and non-institutionalised, inter-generational learning and meeting places.

(2) Open workshops, repair initiatives and community gardens not only serve to organise leisure time in a meaningful way, rather many of its participants are involved productively in social events and make practical and publicly visible contributions to questions such as, "How do we want to design our communities?" and "How do we want to organise local businesses based on local raw materials aiming at long-lasting products which are easy to repair?".

Many initiatives exchange information and learn from each other. In Germany an endowment called "Anstiftung"* is active nationwide. "Anstiften" means "to instigate". The endowment aims to support lifestyle changes, first among minorities and finally reaching the majority of society. It is very concrete and practical. There are for instance webinar offers for building DIY bicycle-powered garden shredders, for producing biochar with a Kon-Tiki or for constructing a wheeled hoe.

Culture

The dying society hindered and prevented cultural activities of all kinds during the last years. In the emerging society we consider culture as a basic component of a healthy social life. Our well-being and our spiritual unfolding are directly dependent upon blossoming culture.

(1) Miha Pogacnik and Adriana von Runic from Slovenia have already organised numerous cultural caravans in crisis and war zones around the world. By doing that they convey courage, strength and inspiration for the post-war and post-crisis period through music and dance.

In March 2022 we had the opportunity to take part in a cultural caravan* in the Balkans. About 15 people around Miha and Adriana formed the solid core of the caravan which moved from Slovenia via Croatia and Bosnia-Herzegovina to Montenegro.

On the way we met hundreds of locals with whom we made music, sang, ate and drank together in monasteries, castles and churches. In a colourful

120

mixture of languages from Slavic languages, English and German, we exchanged news about communities of trust and similar germ cells which are emerging in the countries we visited. There were singing and dancing events with local accordion, fiddle and harp players complementing Miha's wonderful violin playing. Highlights of the caravan were meetings in different emerging trust communities.

(2) The Global Ecovillage Network, an ever-growing network of international communities and ecovillages, performs exciting activities. In 2022 it organised a 6-week bicycle tour* through 40 German eco-villages, places of learning, transition initiatives, regions of change and permaculture projects. Future communities* such as Tempelhof castle, Münsterschwarzach monastery, Cobstädt community, Tonndorf castle, the Sieben Linden eco-village, Gessin community and Klein Jasedow community were stops on the cycle tour. Practical on-site activities and workshops as well as singing and making music together were core elements of this 1,200 km long bike tour from the south to the north of Germany. With saddlebags full of ideas and

examples, the team contacted eco-communities, degrowth initiatives and citizen parliaments. Theatre, art, music, hands-on activities, lectures and workshops took place along the way involving local participants.

Is this an activity you might like to participate in? Or could you imagine organising such a caravan in your region?

Exchange and Regional Currency Systems

A basic problem of the dying society is the interest-based financial system that reinforces social inequality and the unjust distribution of power to people whose activities we have described in the Diagnosis section. Therefore one of the core topics within the emerging society is the creation and installation of alternatives based upon an abundance of experience from history.

In many countries Moslem and Chinese immigrants have their own principles with which they conduct business. It is an informal system based on trust. Creating communities in which the exchange of money and goods is based on trust circumvents the international digital settlement systems which are a controlling mechanism used by the ruling class to exclude certain people.

Solutions can be exchange systems where money is not used. Taking all money out of accounts held in big banks reduces the power of the large corporations. Not using plastic cards (credit cards or debit cards) for payments achieves the same objective. Having accounts in small local banks keeps the money in the local community. Creating local currencies also reduces the power of large corporations and prevents them from obtaining data about you.

The new decentralised financial services include micro-finance, credit unions, crowd funding and local currencies. Many people are already transferring their assets from the large banks to small local banks.

In addition, using cash instead of credit cards also prevents the large financial institutions from growing further and also prevents the large corporations from collecting valuable customer data. Here again, there are plenty of good examples and models we can follow.

(1) In 2010, in response to the economic decline

of the Italian island of Sardinia after the 2008 financial crisis, companies on the island formed a credit club and paid each other for goods and services in "Sardex"*, a local equivalent to the existing global currency systems. The credits are denominated in euros but cannot be exchanged for euros or bought with euros. Transactions are carried out through an online banking site. Currently almost 4,000 companies on the island grant each other interest-free credit via this currency system, independently of banks and the state.

(2) Another example is the WIR Bank* in Switzerland. 60,000 participants move goods worth $2 billion annually without using any of the world currencies! Thomas Greco, a leading expert on moneyless exchange systems, community currencies and community-based economic development, estimates that more than 400,000 companies worldwide move goods and services worth more than $12 billion every year without using an official national currency. Greco's analysis can be found in Silke Helfrich's book on the commons (2012, pp. 178-283).

Finally let us look at some complex approaches of the new society covering several aspects of our future life simultaneously.

(1) In Chiapas and Oaxaca, two federal states in Mexico, regional economy is practised in the following way: *"The families organise their coexistence in their own way. They use traditional practices and modern tools to grow staple foods, coffee and other products that they sell through fair or solidarity trade. Their children go to free "schools" based on community concepts and addressing issues important to the community, such as their own history. They use traditional healing methods, supplemented by their own modern clinics, where they have access to other healing means and methods. They construct their own houses and public buildings using local building materials and according to local traditions, enriched with ideas from other parts of the world."*

That sounds like a fairy tale.... but it is reality. In the volume on the subject of commons by Helfrich (2012, pp. 236-242), Gustavo Esteva reports on the coexistence of indigenous people in the Mexican state of Oaxaca. You can learn from the experiences of these people how local committees make professional politicians superfluous and how family usage rights replace private land ownership.

(2) The tenement syndicate* in Germany, Austria and the Netherlands (Mietshäusersyndikat) is an invention by which the ownership of residential real estate is permanently transferred to the residents and is thus withdrawn from future speculation in the financial casino. If you are curious how this works in detail, look on pages 236-240 in Helfrich's book on the commons (2019).

(3) The agricultural industry is attempting to align plant seeds with profitability and to use legal remedies such as seed licenses to deny the farmers of our world the free use, storage, breeding or repeated sowing of their own seeds.

Not a good idea, according to "La Via Campesina"*, an international network of small farmers, and "Navdanya"*, an organisation founded in India by the winner of the alternative Nobel Prize, Vandana Shiva. The Open Source Seeds initiative*, which emerged in America and the Open Source Seed License Europe initiative* are successfully promoting the understanding of seeds as a life-giving force that must not be perverted for profit by minority economic interests. Are you interested in participating in these worldwide initiatives? You can get or share open source seeds here.

A small book such as this one is not a complete compendium or lexicon. Therefore we have to stop at this point.

After reading about the panoply of global initiatives for our world mentioned on the last pages you are possibly now keen on further details or a systematic summary of such wonderful projects.

If so, take a look at the two legendary open source books by Silke Helfrich and David Bollier. One appeared in 2012 (Helfrich*); The second was published in 2019 (Helfrich & Bollier*). Both books offer contributions by more than one hundred authors from many countries regarding theory and practice of modern concepts of community solutions based on the idea of joint responsibility for common goods.

If you understand German, we invite you to visit our platform portraying 67 future communities*. There you may search for community innovations.

Simply enter your search terms on this platform and find out what is going on in your field of interest in good old Europe.

You can find details on the transition toward new energy sources for the municipal energy on our platform portraying 200 pioneer villages which get heat and electricity with regional resources replacing fossil or nuclear fuels (renewable energy villages*).

For further inspiration regarding the many aspects of the dying and the emerging society we recommend Bernd Senf* (financial aspects, German scientist), Catherine Austin Fitts* ("actionable intelligence to help you live a free and inspired life", financial aspects, former Assistant Housing Secretary in the Bush administration), James Corbett* (Canadian critic of established media and public administration, has a series "Solutions Watch"), Dr Rainer Füllmich* (German lawyer, investigates international crimes), Vandana Shiva (Indian globalisation critic and peace activist, founder of Navdanya*) and Helena Norberg-Hodge (founder of the global ecovillage network and of the local futures initiative*).

Conclusion

The secret of successful evolution is diversity. In this way, suitable designs for a colourful life in the future and for the different desires of people on our planet will emerge from the many innovative social and economic forms we described in the last paragraphs.

It is important that as with all new starts and projects, we show respect for all life and create an economy that serves the common good as the basis of our actions.

Start NOW. Sign few contracts but rather make many agreements based on personal trust and sealed with a handshake.

Good luck in all countries, regions and communities worldwide wherever you and your friends contribute to our emerging society!

Please write to us (peterschmuck@gmx.de, r.grawath@mailfence.com) if you have questions or if you want to share your success stories with our growing international community.

Peter Schmuck and Richard Grawath

Germany and Portugal, March 2023

Further Sources of Information

Below you will find references marked in the book with a * (websites including articles, videos, documents etc.) and scientific references marked in the book with the name of the author and the year of publication (books or scientific articles).

A

Adam, D. (2020). Modelling the Pandemic. *Nature*, Vol 580.

Advratings, BlackRock, Vanguard: *https://www.advratings.com/top-asset-management-firms,* accessed 16th May 2022

Agenda 21: *https://sustainabledevelopment.un.org/content/documents/Agenda21.pdf*, accessed 3rd Jan 2023

Anstiftung Endowment for Repair Initiatives: *https://anstiftung.de/*, accessed 3rd Jan 2023

Arched Cabins: *https://archedcabins.com/*, accessed 3rd Jan 2023

Awake to Paradise: *https://www.awake2paradise.com/*, accessed 3rd Jan 2023

B

Belschner, W. (2007). *Der Sprung in die Transzendenz*. LitVerlag.

Bicycle Courier Service: *https://timmitransport.de/*, accessed 3rd Jan 2023

Bicycle Tour Through Pioneer Communities: *https://gen-deutschland.de/*, accessed 3rd Jan 2023

Blix: UN Inspectors Found No Evidence of Prohibited Weapon Programmes, 5th June 2003, *https://www.un.org/press/en/2003/sc7777.doc.htm,* accessed 3rd Jan 2023

Britannica: Encyclopedia Britannica, *https://www.britannica.com/science/Agent-Orange,* accessed 8th Dec 2022

C

Cobstädt, DIY Windpark: *https://zukunftskommunen.de/blog/einladung-zum-bau-des-vierten-kleinwindrades-in-cobstaedt/*, accessed 3rd Jan 2023

Community Supported Agriculture/CSA: *https://communitysupportedagriculture.org.uk/*, accessed 3rd Jan 2023

Corbett, J.: *https://www.corbettreport.com/,* accessed

3rd Jan 2023

Croft, Ch. (2015). *The Innocence of Kaiser Wilhem II: and the First World War*. Hilliard & Croft.

Cultural Caravans: *https://zukunftskommunen.de/blog/kulturkarawane-auf-dem-balkan-4-13-maerz-2022/*, accessed 3rd Jan 2023

D

Dronninglund: *https://www.dronninglundfjernvarme.dk/media/2985/dronninglund-broschuere-planenergi-deutschpdf.pdf*, accessed 3rd Jan 2023

DW 1: Deutsche Welle 2008, *https://www.dw.com/en/commerzbank-to-tap-germanys-bank-bailout-fund/a-3761170*, accessed 16th May 2022

DW 2: Deutsche Welle 2008, *https://www.dw.com/en/commerzbank-to-speed-up-dresdner-bank-takeover/a-3827821*, accessed 16th May 2022

E

Earth Charter: *https://earthcharter.org/*, accessed 3rd Jan 2023

Earthship: *http://earthship.schloss-tempelhof.de/*, accessed 3rd Jan 2023

Eisenhower (1961) Farewell address by President Dwight D. Eisenhower, *https://www.archives.gov/milestone-documents/president-dwight-d-eisenhowers-farewell-address*, accessed 3rd Jan 2023

F

Fasa AG: *https://aktivsonnenhaus.de/*, accessed 3rd Jan 2023

FBI File about Mountbatten: *https://www.news.com.au/entertainment/celebrity-life/royals/fbi-files-claim-lord-louis-mountbatten-had-a-perversion-for-young-boys/news-story/3647da9b3e938ae4aa5d0f3608639479*, accessed 3rd Jan 2023

Feldheim: *https://zukunftskommunen.de/kommunen-projekte/energieautarkes-dorf-feldheim/*, accessed 3rd Jan 2023

Filling Stations offering compressed natural Biogas: *https://www.biogastankstelle.de/*, accessed 3rd Jan 2023

Fitts, Catherine Austin: *https://solarireport.com*, accessed 3rd Jan 2023

Frankl, V. (1985). *Man's search for meaning*. Simon and Schuster.

Fraiman et al.: *https://www.sciencedirect.com/science/article/pii/S0264410X22010283, accessed 3rd Jan 2023*

Franzen, H. (2001), The Science of the Silver Bullet, Scientific American, *https://www.scientificamerican.com/article/the-science-of-the-silver/,* accessed 3rd Jan 2023

Füllmich, R.: *https://icic.law/en/,* accessed 3rd Jan 2023

Future Communities: *https://zukunftskommunen.de,* accessed 3rd Jan 2023

G

Ganser, D., Die Akademie: *https://dieakademie.org/,* accessed 3rd Jan 2023

Garden Ring Cities: *https://www.gardenringcities.com/,* accessed 3rd Jan 2023

GM: Washington Post, 30. Nov 1998 *https://www.washingtonpost.com/wp-srv/national/daily/nov98/nazicars30.htm,* accessed 3rd Jan 2023

Going direct plan:
https://goingdirect.solari.com/the-going-direct-reset/, accessed 3rd Jan 2023

Grawath, R. (2022a). An Analysis of an Important Text: The World Health Organization's Understanding of Health. ISBN: 978-1-4710-8319-8

Grawath, R. (2022b). Tales of Wisdom and Truth: Modern Life and Voices from the Past. ISBN: 978-1-4717-4695-6

H

Helfrich, S. and Bollier, D. (Eds., 2019): Die Macht der Commons. Transkript-Verlag Bielefeld. *https://www.transcript-verlag.de/978-3-8376-4530-9/frei-fair-und-lebendig-die-macht-der-commons/,* accessed 3rd Jan 2023

Helfrich,S. (Ed., 2012). Commons. Für eine neue Politik jenseits von Markt und Staat. Transkript-Verlag Bielefeld. *https://www.boell.de/sites/default/files/2012-04-buch-2012-04-buch-commons.pdf,* accessed 3rd Jan 2023

Herzkraftwerk Endowment: *https://herzkraftwerk.de/,* accessed 3rd Jan 2023

Höltje, B.: *https://biancahoeltje.de/,* accessed 3rd Jan 2023

House of Commons, UK. Committee of Public Accounts, The Department for Work and Pensions' Accounts 2021–22. Fraud and error in the benefits system, *Twenty-Sixth Report of Session 2022–23*, HC 44, Published on 9 November 2022 by authority of the House of Commons

Huddle, N. (1990). *Butterfly. A Tiny Tale of a Great Transformation*. Washington.

I

IAEA (International Atomic Energy Agency) Topics. Depleted Uranium: *https://www.iaea.org/topics/spent-fuel-management/depleted-uranium*, accessed 3rd Jan 2023

IBM and the Holocaust: *https://de.wikipedia.org/wiki/IBM_und_der_Holocaust*, accessed 3rd Jan 2023

K

Katz, S. The Chemistry and Toxicology of Depleted Uranium. *Toxics*. 2014; 2(1): 50-78. *https://doi.org/10.3390/toxics2010050*

Keiser, F.: *https://zukunftskommunen.de/blog/klimapositive-landwirtschaft-familienbetrieb-keiser-in-der-schweiz-macht-vor-wie-das-geht/*, accessed 3rd Jan 2023

Kern, C.: *https://jurtenbau.at/*, accessed 3rd Jan 2023

Kirchanschöring:
https://zukunftskommunen.de/blog/erstes-ee-regionalwerk-in-deutschland-in-gruendung,
accessed 3rd Jan 2023

Klische, M. (2006). *Transpersonale Entwicklung.*
Universität Duisburg-Essen.

Knittlingerhof Austria:
https://www.knittlingerhof.at/, accessed 3rd Jan 2023

König, M.: *https://www.urstrom.de/macher/*,
accessed 3rd Jan 2023

Kolakowski, L. (1981). Main Currents of Marxism:
Its Rise, Growth, and Dissolution. Clarendon Press.

Köstler, A. (1978). Janus: A Summing Up.
Hutchinson.

L

Lackmann, J.: *https://aende.eu/team/*, accessed 3rd
Jan 2023

La Via Campesina: *https://viacampesina.org/en/*,
accessed 3rd Jan 2023

Lamprecht, J. (2005). *Zur subjektiven Bedeutung
spiritueller Weltanschauungen.* Technical University

Berlin.

Leopold II: BBC News, 13th June 2020
https://www.bbc.com/news/world-europe-53017188,
accessed 3rd Jan 2023

Leppe, Ricardo - Open Source Learning Courses:
https://www.wissenschafftfreiheit.com/kurse/,
accessed 3rd Jan 2023

LIBOR scandal: Jason Fernando, What Was the
Libor Scandal? What Happened and Impacted
Companies.
https://www.investopedia.com/terms/l/libor-
scandal.asp, accessed 3rd Jan 2023

LIFI: *https://zukunftskommunen.de/blog/lifi-vlc-*
gesundheitlich-verantwortbare-alternative-zu-wlan-
in-stuttgart-hamburg-und-auf-mainau-im-einsatz/,
accessed 3rd Jan 2023

Liszt, Daniel: *https://www.darkjournalist.com,*
accessed 3rd Jan 2023

Local Futures Initiative:
https://www.localfutures.org/, accessed 3rd Jan 2023

Lorenzsysteme -Houses from Wood and Straw:
https://lorenzsysteme.de/, accessed 3rd Jan 2023

M

Macgregor, J. & Docherty, G. (2018). *Prolonging the Agony: How The Anglo-American Estabishment Deliberately Extended WWI by Three-and-a-Half Years*. Walterville. Trine Day LLC.

Maxwell, G.: *https://www.justice.gov/usao-sdny/pr/ghislaine-maxwell-sentenced-20-years-prison-conspiring-jeffrey-epstein-sexually-abuse,* accessed 3rd Jan 2023

McNamara: U.S. Didn't Belong in Vietnam, Chicago Tribune, 9th Apr 1995, *https://www.chicagotribune.com/news/ct-xpm-1995-04-09-9504090201-story.html,* accessed 3rd Jan 2023

Mills, C. and Dempsey, N., (2022) The Cost of the UK's Strategic Nuclear Deterrent, *https://commonslibrary.parliament.uk/research-briefings/cbp-8166/,* accessed 3rd Jan 2023

Mountbatten, L., 1st Earl Mountbatten of Burma: *https://en.wikipedia.org/wiki/Louis_Mountbatten,_1st_Earl_Mountbatten_of_Burma*, accessed 19th May 2022

N

Navdanya: *https://www.navdanya.org/*, accessed 3rd Jan 2023

Nbcnews, 2013: Iraq War 10 Years Later: *https://www.nbcnews.com/news/world/iraq-war-10-years-later-where-are-they-now-mohammed-flna1C8956472*, accessed 3rd Jan 2023

New Earth Manifesto: *https://thenewearthmanifesto.com/en/*, accessed 3rd Jan 2023

O

Oberrosphe: *https://www.bioenergiedorf-oberrosphe.de/*, accessed 3rd Jan 2023

Open Source Seeds initiative: *https://www.opensourceseeds.org/*, accessed 3rd Jan 2023

Open Source Seeds initiative in Europe: *https://www.opensourceseeds.org/en/open-source-seed-licence*, accessed 3rd Jan 2023

Operation Unthinkable: *https://www.nationalarchives.gov.uk/education/resources/cold-war-on-file/operation-unthinkable/*, accessed 3rd Jan 2023

Otterpohl, R. (2017). *Das neue Dorf*. Oekom.

Otterpohl, R. (2022). *Neues Dorf für Neue Erde*. Epubli Verlag. (English version: Otterpohl, R. and Toth, A., Garden Communities. Living diversely, producing locally, together with nature and neighbors, actually in print).

P

Permaculture/bio-intensive cultivation: *https://www.fermedubec.com/*, *https://zukunftskommunen.de/blog/ferme-du-bec-frankreich-permakultur-rechnet-sich/*, accessed 3rd Jan 2023

Penndorf, T.: *https://zukunftskommunen.de/kommunen-projekte/arche-cobstedt/*, accessed 3rd Jan 2023

Perpignan/LIFI network: *https://yewtu.be/watch?v=Cx9yUzXglHU*, accessed 3rd Jan 2023

R

Reetz village: *https://zukunftskommunen.de/blog/ackerland-in-buergerhand-der-verein-oelala-im-flaeming-brandenburg/*, accessed 3rd Jan 2023

Renewable Energy Villages: *https://.energiewendedörfer.de*, accessed 3rd Jan 2023

Repair Cafés: *https://www.repaircafe.org/en/*, accessed 3rd Jan 2023

S

Sardex: *https://monneta.org/en/sardex/*, accessed 3rd
Jan 2023

Savile 1:
https://en.wikipedia.org/wiki/Jimmy_Savile,
accessed 19th May 2022

Savile 2:
*https://en.wikipedia.org/wiki/Jimmy_Savile_sexual_
abuse_scandal*, accessed 19th May 2022

Schmuck, P. & Sheldon, K. (Eds.) (2001). *Life goals
and well-being. Towards a positive psychology of
human striving*. Seattle: Hogrefe & Huber.

Schmuck, P. (2013). The Göttingen Approach of
Sustainability Science: Creating Renewable Energy
Communities in Germany and Testing a Psycholo-
gical Hypothesis. *Umweltpsychologie*, 17, 119-135.

Schmuck, P. (2015). *Die Kraft der Vision. Plädoyer
für eine neue Denk- und Lebenskultur*. München:
OEKOM Verlag.

Schmuck, P. (2017). Von der Umweltpsychologie zu
einer Transformationspsychologie der Potential-
entfaltung. *Umweltpsychologie*, 21, 106-118.

Senf, B.: *http://berndsenf.de/*, accessed 3rd Jan 2023

Siedle, E. (2022) Blackboxes within Blackboxes,

Crypto-Currency in your State Pension: *https://www.forbes.com/sites/edwardsiedle/2022/11/28/blackboxes-within-blackboxes-cryptocurrency-in-your-state-pension/*, accessed 14th January 2023

Solar Heating Villages: *https://zukunftskommunen.de/blog/acht-solarenergiedoerfer-in-deutschland-2018/*, accessed 3rd Jan 2023

Solar Island: *https://zukunftskommunen.de/blog/krisensicherer-pv-strom-mit-solarinseln/*, accessed 3rd Jan 2023

SoLaWi communities: *https://www.solidarische-landwirtschaft.org/startseite*, accessed 3rd Jan 2023

Statisticstimes: Projected GDP Ranking, *https://statisticstimes.com/economy/projected-world-gdp-ranking.php*, access 16th May 2022

Surdyk, S, Itani, M., Al-Lobaidy, M. et al. (2021). Weaponised Uranium and Adverse Health Outcomes in Iraq: A Systematic Review. *British Medical Journal, Global Health*, 6, pp. 1-102.

T

Tenement Syndicate: *https://www.syndikat.org/der-projektverbund/*, accessed 3rd Jan 2023

U

US Department of Veteran Affairs, Exposures:
Depleted Uranium,
https://www.publichealth.va.gov/exposures/depleted_uranium/, accessed 8th Dec 2022

V

Von Carlowitz, Hans Carl:
https://en.wikipedia.org/wiki/Hans_Carl_von_Carlowitz, accessed 3rd Jan 2023

Von Meding, J., October 4, 2017:
https://theconversation.com/agent-orange-exposed-how-u-s-chemical-warfare-in-vietnam-unleashed-a-slow-moving-disaster-84572, accessed 3rd Jan 2023

W

Wagner, F. (2007). Deadly Dust: Depleted Uranium:
https://yewtu.be/watch?v=kLuR8UGco6k, accessed 4th Nov 2021

Wellerstein, A., 4th August 2020, Counting the Dead at Hiroshima and Nagasaki:
https://thebulletin.org/2020/08/counting-the-dead-at-hiroshima-and-nagasaki/, accessed 27th May 2022

WikiHouse Open Source Platform:
https://www.wikihouse.cc/, accessed 3rd Jan 2023

WIR Bank/Switzerland: *https://www.wir.ch/de/die-bank-wir/ueber-uns*, accessed 3rd Jan 2023

Wohnwagon - Tiny Houses:
https://wohnwagon.at/der-wohnwagon/, accessed 3rd Jan 2023

About the Authors

Peter Schmuck is a psychologist, lecturer, researcher and new world activist. He conducted research at several German and Austrian universities on the potentials of people engaging in new, fair and clean ways of life. With collaborators and students he has interviewed thousands of people who have set out to discover and develop their potentials and have contributed to new ways of living.

He contributed to the development of new ways of living with respect to the production and distribution of local energy. With colleagues from the University of Göttingen he initiated 200 villages in Germany in taking over ownership and management of their domestic energy supply. Today these villages use local energy resources such as wind, solar power and bio-energy.

His professional experience as a researcher spans over four decades. Many of his 120 scientific publications analyse human potentials or describe success factors of building new communities replacing the dying socio-economic structure.

Richard Grawath worked as a banker for American Express Bank, Deutsche Bank and Hauck Private Bank and then as a strategic management consultant for Watson Wyatt in the UK. He also lectured at NTT University and Hoa Sen University in Vietnam and conducted medical research amongst i.a., in conjunction with the Directorate for Health Information & Research in Malta.

His professional qualification as a banker (Bankkaufmann, State Chamber of Commerce) was followed by several further qualifications: Postgraduate Diploma in Medical Physics, M.Sc. in Science, M.B.A., Diploma in Psychology, B.Sc. (Honours) in Health Studies, B.Sc. (Honours) in Health & Social Care, University Certificate in Managing Care, University Certificate in Promoting Health, University Certificate in Reflective and Evidence-Based Practice, University Certificate in Health & Social Care.

His academic and professional background provides the basis for his work on ethics, medical global statistical indicators and global power centres such as the World Health Organization.